READABILITY REVISITED
The New Dale-Chall Readability Formula

Readability Revisited

The New Dale-Chall Readability Formula

Jeanne S. Chall

Edgar Dale

Brookline Books

Cover design by Crane Graphics, Canton, MA.
Book design by Erica Schultz.
Printed in USA by McNaughton & Gunn, Inc., Saline, MI.

ISBN 1-57129-008-7

Library of Congress Cataloging-In-Publication Data
Chall, Jeanne Sternlicht, 1921–
    Readability revisited : the new Dale-Chall readability formula /
Jeanne S. Chall, Edgar Dale.
        p.   cm.
    Includes bibliographical references and index.
    ISBN 1-57129-008-7 (pbk.)
    1. Textbooks--Readability. 2. Readability (Literary style)
I. Dale, Edgar, 1900-1985. II. Title.
LB3045.8.C466 1995
371.3'2--dc20   95-16034
                                                           CIP

Published by
Brookline Books
P.O. Box 1047 • Cambridge, Massachusetts 02238-1047

Contents

PREFACE

We are most grateful to many of our colleagues and coworkers for their assistance with various aspects of this work. We extend special thanks to John Bormuth, Edmund Coleman, Walter MacGinitie and Thomas Sticht, key researchers in readability measurement, who made the basic data for their readability formulas available to us. We also gratefully acknowledge the assistance of Walter MacGinitie in the use of the standardization data for the Gates-MacGinitie Tests in our cross-validation studies; the use of Ted Kilty's data on the readability of numbers; and the exchange of many useful ideas with George Klare.

The new formula owes a great debt to the dedicated work of Sue Conard on all aspects of the book, and to Dorothy Henry and Andrea Kotula for the various readability analyses.

We are most appreciative for the work of Marcus Lieberman, our statistical consultant; of Joseph O'Rourke, who assisted in developing the new word list and who read the first draft; and of Vicki Jacobs, who helped us with the bibliography.

To Ann Cura and Elizabeth Chapin, who worked on the early versions of this manuscript with care and dedication, we extend our warmest thanks and appreciation.

Edgar Dale, Columbus, Ohio
Jeanne S. Chall, Cambridge, Mass.
January 1984

The above preface was completed by Edgar Dale and myself in January 1984. It was to be used with an earlier draft of the present book.

Unfortunately, Edgar Dale died on March 8, 1985, before he could see the book in print. He had looked forward to its publication as a kind of culmination of our combined work in readability, which started in 1948, as well as his own work on vocabulary and simple writing.

The present book contains many changes. It includes separate chapters on the classic and new cognitive-structural approaches to readability, and a comparison of these. The background literature has been updated, and the chapters have been reorganized to make the work more readable to various groups — practitioners, researchers, and theorists.

The revised Dale-Chall formula remains as Edgar Dale and I developed it in the early 1980s. The qualitative judgment of various cognitive-structural aspects of text difficulty have been added within the past year.

Edgar Dale looked forward to the publication of this book. To him, readability was much more than a research tool. It was a way to extend education and understanding to ever larger numbers of people, and in so doing, to make us all more knowledgeable and more humane.

I should like to thank Rebekah Wolman, Martha Smith, Andrea Kotula and Ruth Litchfield for their work on various aspects of the book, and Karen Reiferson, Elizabeth Purswell, Mitra Shavarini and Sharon Hibbert for their careful work on the revised draft.

Jeanne S. Chall
February 1995

INTRODUCTION

The book has several purposes. It presents the new Dale-Chall Readability Formula with full instructions for its use, statistical and theoretical evidence of its validity, and how it is best used. It also compares the new formula with the original Dale-Chall formula and other readability measures developed over a period of about 70 years.

It describes and compares the two major readability paradigms — the classic readability formulas that predict readability mainly through semantic and syntactic factors, and the new cognitive-structural readability measures that rely mainly on cognitive and organizational features of text.

A final section is concerned with writing readable and clear text and presents suggestions broadly derived from readability research and from a long literary tradition.

The Plan of the Book

The book is divided into four sections. The first section (Chapters 1, 2 and 3) presents the new Dale-Chall Readability Formula. Chapter 1 introduces the Dale-Chall formula — the purposes for which it was originally developed, its uses over the years, and the purposes behind the present revision. The chapter also places the formula in a historical and theoretical context — within what we call the classic paradigm.

Chapter 2 presents the data and instructions for using the new formula. These include an updated Dale list of the 3,000 words familiar to 4th graders and various tables for computing readability scores. The new formula includes instructions for making qualitative assessments of cognitive and structural variables and for estimating the reading abilities, interest and other relevant features of the targeted readers.

Chapter 3 focuses on the proper and improper uses of the new formula and the meaning and interpretation of the readability scores.

Section II (Chapters 4 and 5) presents the scientific basis of the new formula. Chapter 4 presents the basic standardization data, and Chapter 5 presents the results of comparing the new readability scores with the difficulty scores from various independent measures.

Section III (Chapters 6, 7 and 8) presents a theoretical and research perspective on the two readability paradigms. Chapter 6 presents classic readability — its theories, research, and uses over a period of more than seventy years. Chapter 7 presents the cognitive-structural paradigm — the theories, research and uses of the newer readability procedures proposed during the past 15 years by linguists and cognitive psychologists. Chapter 8 presents a synthesis of the two paradigms.

Section IV (Chapters 9 and 10) focuses on the practical uses of readability measurement. Chapter 9 suggests how word lists may be used to measure readability and to develop readable materials. Chapter 10 presents suggestions for writing clearly and simply that are based broadly on readability principles and on a long literary tradition.

Section I

THE DALE-CHALL READABILITY FORMULA: AN INTRODUCTION TO THE ORIGINAL AND THE NEW FORMULAS

This section (Chapters 1, 2 and 3) focuses on the new Dale-Chall Readability Formula. Chapter 1 begins with an introduction and historical overview of the original formula — its purposes, various uses over the years, and how it fits in with other measures of readability — the classic and the cognitive-structural paradigms.

Chapter 2 presents the instructions and worksheets for using the new formula, together with the updated Dale list of 3,000 words familiar to 4th graders, and various tables for computing the readability scores. The chapter also contains suggestions and guidelines for assessing cognitive and organizational aspects of text difficulty. Also included in the instructions are suggestions for estimating characteristics of prospective readers of a text — their reading ability, their prior relevant knowledge, their interest in the text, how they will be using it, and what they are expected to get out of it.

Chapter 3 includes suggestions on how the new formula and others like it are best used — the kind of materials they evaluate well and the kind they do not. It also considers the meaning of the various readability scores, how they are to be interpreted, and presents some guidelines for optimal "matching" of readers to printed and oral texts.

CHAPTER 1

The Original Dale-Chall Formula

The Dale-Chall Readability Formula, one of the classic approaches to readability measurement, has been used to estimate the difficulty of written and spoken materials for more than forty years. First published in 1948, it soon became one of the most widely used formulas for predicting the difficulty of reading materials — particularly textbooks and other educational materials. For several decades, it was acknowledged to be the most popular readability formula in educational circles (Klare, 1988). Its predictions of comprehension difficulty were also reported to be the most valid when compared to independent measures of comprehension difficulty — such as multiple choice and cloze tests, teachers' and/or students' judgments of difficulty, and other accepted measures of reading comprehension — and when compared to other classic formulas (Klare, 1988). Thus it was not a surprise that Frances Fitzgerald used it as a prototype in her examination of the uses and misuses of readability by educational publishers (Fitzgerald, 1979).

Through the years following its publication, the authors monitored the formula's use in research and in practice. We were particularly interested in evidence of its reliability and validity, knowing that the appeal and popularity of the formula stemmed, in part, from its great simplicity — the use of only two factors to predict difficulty: word familiarity and syntactic complexity. We were aware that we had traded accuracy for greater simplicity, hoping that the trade-off did not result in too great a loss of predictive validity.

The review of readability research and application by Chall in 1958 confirmed that the formula was valid for predicting readers' ability to comprehend text, to read it at an adequate rate, and to judge its difficulty. It was also a useful predictor of the level of difficulty of standardized reading tests.

In spite of the formula's high validity and the positive feedback from a survey of early users (Chall, 1956), we began to discuss a revision in 1960. Based on a literature review of the readability research and its applications (Chall, 1958), we proposed two kinds of revisions: first, a refinement of the original formula by using a new set of criterion passages[1], an updated word list, and better rules for measuring the two factors of word familiarity and sentence length; second, a simplification

---

[1] Readability formulas are developed by using a set of materials that have been tested for difficulty by an independent measure such as a test of reading comprehension, rate of reading, or judgments of difficulty. These are called criterion passages.

of the instructions and computations.

In addition, we wished to include more information on how the readability scores were to be interpreted, particularly in relation to readers of varying abilities, backgrounds, and interests.

We also wished to make greater provision for measuring conceptual difficulties, especially when they are not captured by the count of unfamiliar words, as well as the influence of text cohesion and organization on passage difficulty.

From the early 1960s to the late 1970s, a considerable correspondence passed between the two authors as to whether or not we should revise the formula since it was so widely used and accepted. Also, other responsibilities of both authors kept us from starting the work. But equally influential was the concern that a revision would not necessarily improve the instrument. After all, the original formula promised only an estimate of difficulty, and it seemed to be fulfilling this promise well. Indeed, there were sufficient examples from standardized testing that revisions are not necessarily improvements over the originals. Therefore, we were cautious about undertaking a revision.

By the late 1970s we were convinced that it was time for a revision, and we set out to make the refinements and improvements noted above. The major revisions were completed during the early 1980s; the resulting new formula was tried out in various research projects and in readability assessments at the Harvard Reading Laboratory.

The manuscript was almost completed in 1985 when Edgar Dale died. When I was able to continue the work, considerable changes had occurred in the literature on readability — in the research and in the discussion. Indeed, the 1980s and early 1990s seemed to bring a new paradigm to readability — one that looked toward cognitive and structural factors. The new readability researchers came mainly from linguistics and cognitive psychology. Some of them proposed different schemes for measuring the comprehension difficulty of texts — schemes based not on semantic and syntactic measures but on such features as cohesion, idea density, and relationships between ideas. Indeed, many who proposed cognitive and structural approaches to readability tended to be quite critical of classic readability. However, some combined the classic with the cognitive-structural measures. (See Chapters 6, 7 and 8 for a fuller discussion of the two readability paradigms.)

Criticism of classic readability came also from students of children's literature. They claimed that the misuse of classic readability formulas by educational publishers led to the poor quality of stories included in elementary level reading textbooks and literature anthologies. They said that textbook publishers selected stories for reading textbooks and literature anthologies to fit given formula scores. Hence the textbooks tended to omit more difficult stories of quality. It was suggested, instead, that literary quality and child appeal guide the selection of stories, without concern for difficulty (see Cullinan & Fitzgerald, 1984). A new term was coined: *formularized books*, which were said to be written or selected to meet desired readability scores rather than curricula or quality standards.

In spite of the considerable criticism of the classic readability measures during the 1980s and early 1990s, there seemed to be an increase in their use. There were an increasing number of computer programs on the market for analyzing text difficulty using one or more of the classic readability formulas.

Several new readability formulas were developed and used about the same time. A classic readability formula based on highly sophisticated statistical procedures, Lexile Theory, was developed in the late 1980s (Stenner, Horabin, Smith & Smith, 1988). The Degrees of Reading Power, a modified cloze reading test developed in the late 1970s, used a classic readability measure, the Bormuth, which contains the two factors from the original Dale-Chall (unfamiliar words and sentence length) and an added word length factor. Other recently published standardized reading tests also use classic readability measures to select passages of increasing difficulty (see Chapter 4, this volume).

The criticisms of the 1980s and early 1990s, perhaps the strongest since the beginnings of readability measurement in the early 1920s, did not seem to reduce interest in and use of classic readability measurement. The number of computer programs available for the classic readability formulas increased. During the past several years we have received many calls from book and test publishers and computer companies asking when the new Dale-Chall formula will be available. During the period of strong negative views on classic readability measurement, Edward Fry (1989) wrote that in spite of the criticisms, the research evidence has consistently found the classic readability measures to be valid.

During the late 1970s, most teachers and publishers noted that they used readability formulas and principles in the selection of textbooks. By the late 1980s, however, few teachers and publishers noted wide use of readability formulas. Although they did express interest in readability, they said they used other words for it: comprehensibility of a text, its style, its quality and its interest to students. Also, the readability levels of the books published in the late 1980s did not change, grade for grade, when compared to the readability of textbooks published during the 1970s when readability formulas were widely used. The consistency of readability scores from the 1970s to the 1980s suggests that the use of readability measurement continued in spite of the use of different terms to describe it (Chall & Conard, 1991).

Further evidence that the classic readability formulas are still in wide use as indices of difficulty is their incorporation into computer programs designed to assess the effectiveness of writing and as a guide for writing and editing. One of the earliest of these (Frase, 1980) uses word and sentence factors, the main factors in classic readability, along with other aspects of readability to help writers estimate the difficulty of their writing and how to improve it. Some of the newer computer programs include spelling checks and other features.

Classic readability formulas are also used in computer programs designed to teach writing by "feeding back" to the students the kinds of words and sentences they use — and helping them increase the maturity of their writing by encouraging the use of less familiar words and longer sentences. Thus, it would seem that although criticism of classic readability measurement has been considerable, it is still very much in use. But this does not mean that the criticisms of classic readability measures have no merit, nor that the cognitive-structural approaches have little to offer. Indeed, after studying the various approaches — the classic and the new cognitive-structural approaches — it would seem that we are dealing with two paradigms — two approaches to readability measurement, each with its particular strengths and weaknesses. (See Chapters 6, 7 and 8.)

While there is merit in the newer cognitive-structural paradigm, it does not mean that the classic measures should be abandoned. Indeed, the position taken in this book is that each has merit and that ultimately the important features of each can be combined to develop procedures for measuring text difficulty that will be superior to either one alone. We have attempted to do so in the pages that follow.

Chapter 2

Instructions for Using the New Dale-Chall Formula

An Overview of Readability Measurement

It should be remembered that readability formulas estimate difficulty on the basis of the factors that have the highest prediction of difficulty. What makes readability measures work is that in natural language, the various factors tend to be related in a similar way to independent measures of text difficulty. Thus, when one writes simple texts—for either children or adults who have limited reading ability—one tends to write about familiar topics, using familiar words, short sentences, and simple organization.

Most of the classic readability formulas have found the strongest predictor of overall text difficulty to be word difficulty—whether measured as word frequency, familiarity, or word length. One of these factors is usually sufficient for accurate measurement, since most word factors are also related to each other (Chall, 1958; Chall & Conard, 1991; Klare, 1963 and 1984). That word length and word difficulty was highly related was demonstrated by the noted philologist George Kingsley Zipf (1935), who found that for all alphabetic languages the common, more concrete, easier words tended to be the shorter words. He further showed that when longer words are used frequently, they tend to become shorter, e.g., *television* to *TV* in the US and *telly* in Britain.

The next best predictor of comprehension difficulty in classic readability formulas is sentence length. Sentence length stands up quite well as a predictor of syntactic complexity—even better than more complex syntactic measures based on sophisticated linguistic theories. (See Bormuth, 1971, and MacGinitie & Tretiak, 1971.)

Once words and sentences are used in a readability formula, little is usually gained by adding other word and sentence factors to the formula. (See, however, the Bormuth formula, 1964, which uses two word difficulty factors: word length and unfamiliar words, according to the original Dale-Chall formula.) Such word features as concreteness versus abstractness also distinguish easy from hard texts and tend to give similar results as an easy/hard vocabulary continuum. For example, the chances are great that words judged to be concrete would be on the Dale list of 3,000 words known by 4th graders. Those not on the list would generally be judged to be more abstract.

No readability formula is a complete and full measure of text difficulty. It measures only a limited number of the many characteristics that make text easy or hard to read and understand. An awareness of these limitations will lead to a wiser and more satisfactory use of readability measures. Hopefully, it will avoid a mechanical approach that can lead to disappointment.

The New Dale-Chall Formula

The new Dale-Chall formula is based on the two most potent factors in classic readability measurement: semantic (word) difficulty, and syntactic (sentence) difficulty. These two, together, correlate .92 with reading comprehension as determined by cloze comprehension scores[1].

The greater predictive power of the new formula stems from several sources: a new set of criterion passages that uses cloze procedure for estimating comprehension difficulty, an updated word list, and improved rules for counting words as familiar or unfamiliar. Other changes in the new formula include a choice for reporting text difficulty—either as cloze scores[2] or as reading levels[3].

The new Dale-Chall formula provides guidelines for making an optimal match between texts and readers by estimating reading abilities of the intended audience, their background knowledge, motivation, purposes for reading, and the availability of assistance from teachers or knowledgeable peers. The new formula also suggests ways to make judgments about the influence of cognitive-structural factors on the reading difficulty of written text.

Guidelines are also presented in the following pages for interpreting the formula scores for use in research and practice. Sample selections from a variety of texts at different levels of difficulty are included in Appendix B to illustrate the various readablity scores.

An Overview of the Instructions for Using the New Dale-Chall Formula

Instructions for selecting samples, for counting sentences and unfamiliar words, and for obtaining cloze and reading level scores are given on the following pages.

---

[1] In the original formula, the word and sentence factors together correlated .70 with reading comprehension.
[2] Cloze scores are the number of correct inserts out of 100 deleted words. The higher the cloze scores, the easier the text.
[3] Reading levels are the approximate reading ability levels for reading and understanding the text. The higher the reading level, the harder the text.

Worksheet A on page 9 is used for recording the basic data and the readability scores for each of the samples and for the entire text.

Worksheet B, page 10, contains instructions for judging reader characteristics and for recording them.

Worksheet C, page 11, contains instructions for making judgments about the cognitive-structural aspects of text and for recording them.

General Instructions

1. Enter all identifying information before the analysis.

2. *Selecting Exact 100-Word Samples.* For each sample, record the page number and note the words that begin and end the sample. To select an exact 100-word sample, begin with the first word in a sentence, and count to 100. Include any headings that fall within the sample.

- *For books of 150 pages or longer,* select one sample systematically from every 50th page, starting near the beginning, and systematically thereafter from every 50th page.
- *For books of 5 to 150 pages,* select 3 samples from the beginning, middle, and end. Do *not* use opening or closing pages, since these tend to be easier or harder than the rest of the text. If the writing style is not even, select 4 or 5 samples.
- *For selections of 4 pages or less,* select 2 samples—one near the beginning and one near the end, but not exactly the beginning or end.

3. Record the number of *complete sentences* on Worksheet A. (See p. 12 for specific instructions).
4. Record the number of *unfamiliar words* on Worksheet A. (See more specific instructions on pp. 13-15).
5. Obtain the *Cloze Score* (see Table 2-1, pp. 30-37) by reading the number of unfamiliar words (on the left) and the number of sentences (on top). Record the score for each sample on Worksheet A.
6. Obtain the *Reading Level* (see Table 2-2, pp. 38-44) by reading the number of unfamiliar words (on the left) and the number of sentences (on top). Record the level for each sample on Worksheet A.

Repeat for each sample, then obtain *Average Cloze Scores* and *Reading Levels.* Record on Worksheet A.
7. Judge and record reader characteristics (Worksheet B).
8. Judge and record the cognitive and structural aspects of text (Worksheet C).

Shorter Samples

For samples shorter than 100 words, e.g., test items or brief instructions:

Turn the number of sentences into a percentage — that is, prorate to 100 words. Use the following formula:

$$\frac{\text{sentences}}{\text{words in selection}} \quad = \quad \begin{array}{l}\text{number of sentences}\\\text{in 100 word sample}\end{array}$$

Example: A sample of 60 words and 3 sentences converts to 5 sentences per 100 words.

Turn the number of unfamiliar words into a percentage — that is, prorate to 100 words. Use the following formula:

$$\frac{\text{unfamiliar words}}{\text{words in selection}} \quad = \quad \begin{array}{l}\text{number of unfamiliar words}\\\text{in 100-word sample}\end{array}$$

Example: A sample of 60 words with 5 unfamiliar words converts to 8 unfamiliar words per 100 words.

Use the tables on pages 30-44 to obtain Cloze and/or Reading Level scores.

Assessing Several Aspects of Readability

The new Dale-Chall readability scores are to be recorded on Worksheet A.

To broaden the overall judgment of optimal difficulty for readers of given reading ability, background knowledge and purpose, Worksheets B and C are suggested.

To obtain a more complete view of the match between the reader and the text, all three Worksheets should be examined.

SPECIFIC INSTRUCTIONS FOR USING THE NEW DALE-CHALL READABILITY FORMULA

1. *Counting the Number of Words in a Sample*
Words commonly considered words are to be counted as such.

a. *Count the following as one word*:

- Hyphenated words and contractions
  Example: *lady-in-waiting* is counted as one word.
  don't is one word.
  (Do not include words hyphenated because of syntax. Thus, words like *task-relevant* and *anxiety-provoking* are counted as two words each.)

THE NEW DALE-CHALL READABILITY FORMULA
WORKSHEET A

1.

Book or Article _____

Source _____

Publisher _____

Date of Publication _____

Analyzed by _____

Date of Analysis_____

		2		3	4	5	6
	Page Number	From	To	Number of Sentences	Number of Unfamiliar Words	Cloze Score (From Table 2-1)	Reading Level (From Table 2-2)
Sample 1							
Sample 2							
Sample 3							
Sample 4							
Sample 5							
Sample 6							
Sample 7							
Sample 8							
						Average of Cloze Scores	Average Reading Level

THE NEW DALE-CHALL READABILITY FORMULA
WORKSHEET B

Judging Reader Characteristics

After applying the new Dale-Chall readability formula, make an assessment of the reading abilities of the intended readers.

For assessing reading abilities, use the reading levels from a reading achievement test, last school grade achieved, or the estimated level of books or magazines that are read by the prospective readers. Make an educated guess if objective data are not available.

In general, if the material is to be read independently, it should be at or below the readers' reading level. If the material is to be used for instructional purposes aided by teacher instruction, it can be on the readers' level or on a higher level.

Approximate Average Reading Level _____ Range _____

How were reading levels determined? _____ by tests _____ estimated

How is the material to be used? Check one or more:

_____ For independent reading

_____ For instruction, with little teacher assistance

_____ For instruction, with much teacher assistance

Are prospective readers likely to be interested in the topic? _____ yes _____ no

Comments _____

_____

_____

Are they likely to be interested in the way the topic is presented? ___ yes ___ no

Comments _____

_____

_____

THE NEW DALE-CHALL READABILITY FORMULA
WORKSHEET C

Judging Cognitive-Structural Aspects of Text

Estimate whether the text organization, its conceptual difficulty and density, and its format may make the text more difficult, less difficult, or about the same as that predicted by the new Dale-Chall Readability Formula.

For each of the following characteristics, the analyst is to judge whether it probably raises, lowers, or leaves unchanged the readability estimates obtained from the formula.

Compared with the new Dale-Chall readability scores, check the following:

	Less readable	More readable	About the same
The *prior knowledge* expected of the reader seems to make the text	_____	_____	_____

(For example, consider the following: Does the text require more or less background knowledge than assumed by the author of the text? Is much of the new information unexplained, requiring that readers already know much of what is stated, or can they make the needed inferences?)

The *vocabulary and concepts* used in the text seem to make the text	_____	_____	_____

(For example, are the unfamiliar concepts and words in the text defined, explained, and used in a rich context that will make it readable for the intended readers?)

The *overall organization* seems to make the text	_____	_____	_____

(For example, is the text clearly organized? Do the ideas follow logically from one another?)

The use of *headings, questions, illustrations* and *physical features* seem to make the text	_____	_____	_____

(For example, do the headings and other physical features highlight important information for the reader? Are questions used in a manner that helps the reader remember what is read? Do the illustrations help explain new and difficult ideas? Are the captions meaningful? Are the illustrations placed near the text they are to illustrate?)

- Numerals
  Example: *10* is one word.
             1978 is one word.
             1,000,000 is one word.

- Compound names of persons and places
  Example: *St. John* is one word.
             Van Buren is one word.
             del Rio is one word.
  (However, *New York* and *New England* are counted as two words each.)

- Initials in names of persons are part of the surname.
  Example: *Elizabeth B. Browning* counts as two words.
             T. S. Eliot counts as one word.

- Abbreviations, initials, and acronyms
  Example: *Y.W.C.A.* is counted as one word.
             A.M. and *P.M.* count as one word each.
             J.F.K. is counted as one word.
             NOW is counted as one word.

b. *Count the following as separate words*:

- Each word in the name of an organization, law, or title
  Example: *Declaration of Independence* is counted as three words.
             American Automobile Association is three words.
             A Tale of Two Cities is counted as five words.

- Each word in place names
  Example: *Empire State Building* is counted as three words.
             Twenty-third Avenue is counted as two words
             McDonald's Restaurant is counted as two words.
             Miller's Pond is counted as two words.

2. *Count the Number of Sentences*:
For exact 100-word samples, count *only* the number of complete sentences.

- Count as complete sentences those that end in a period, question, or exclamation mark. (Semi-colons and colons are not considered to be sentence breaking markers.)

- Topic headings are counted as sentences, even when they contain no punctuation or contain only one word.

A SPECIAL NOTE ON COUNTING UNFAMILIAR WORDS:
It is well to remember that words *on* the list of 3,000 words are known to 80 percent of students in 4th grade. These words may be viewed as the most elemental words in the English language — words about home, family, food, clothing, emotions, etc. Generally, these words and their meanings are known without formal schooling. Most words *not* on the list can be thought of as "educated" words, those usually learned in school from about 4th grade on, and primarily from reading. Usually these are specialized, technical, abstract, or literary words.

We suggest that the analyst make a first approximation as to whether a word is familiar ("elemental") or unfamiliar ("educated"). The list (and guidelines) should then be consulted to confirm the analyst's judgment. With practice this procedure becomes quite rapid.

3. *Count the Unfamiliar Words*:
Underline all unfamiliar words as many times as they appear, except for "unfamiliar" names and places. Unfamiliar names and places are counted only once in a sample.

a. *Count the following as familiar words*:

- All words on the new Dale List of 3,000 words, including variations noted in parentheses.

- Regular plurals and possessives of words on the list (*-'s, -s, -es, -ies*).
  Example: *boy's* is familiar because *boy* is on the list.
  girls is familiar because *girl* is on the list.
  churches is familiar because *church* is on the list.
  armies is familiar because *army* is on the list.
  Note: *Irregular plurals*, if *not* on the list or in parentheses, are counted *unfamiliar*.
  Example: *oxen* is unfamiliar even though *ox* is on the list (irregular plural).

- Words on the list with the following endings:

  -d, -ed, -ied.
  Examples: *voted* is familiar because *vote* is on the list.
  tripped is familiar because *trip* is on the list.
  carried is familiar because *carry* is on the list.

  -ing.
  Examples: *doing* is familiar because *do* is on the list.
  dropping is familiar because *drop* is on the list.

  -s, -es, -ies.
  Examples: *works* is familiar because *work* is on the list.

guesses is familiar because *guess* is on the list.
worries is familiar because *worry* is on the list.

-r, -er, -est, -ier, -iest.
Examples: *dancer* is familiar because *dance* is on the list.
longer is familiar because *long* is on the list.
bravest is familiar because *brave* is on the list.
prettier is familiar because *pretty* is on the list.
happiest is familiar because *happy* is on the list.

Note: Count a word unfamiliar if two or more endings are added to a word on the list, e.g., *clippings* (*-ing* + *-s*).

• Compound and hyphenated words on the list are counted familiar if both components are on the list. (They are counted *unfamiliar* if one or both components are *not* on the list.)
Example: *firelight* is considered familiar because *fire* and *light* are listed.

b.   *Count the following as unfamiliar words:*

• Words not on the list.

• Words on the list with the following endings: *-tion, -ation, -ment, -ly, -y.*

• Hyphenated and compound words that are not on the list or if one or both components are not listed.
Example: *will-of-the-wisp* is counted as one unfamiliar word, since *wisp* is not on the list.
work-oriented is counted as one unfamiliar word, since *work* is on the list but *orient* is not.
(Count as two unfamiliar words if both are not on the list.)

• Proper names and places not on the list. *But count unfamiliar only once in a 100-word sample.*

GUIDELINES FOR NUMERALS
The formula is not intended to measure the readability of texts whose content is primarily mathematical. However, for texts with occasional use of numbers, the following guidelines[4] are suggested.

i. Count as familiar the following:

---

[4] These guidelines are adapted, with the generous permission of the author, the late Dr. Ted K. Kilty, who tested these mathematical terms on children in the fourth grade. For the complete research, see Kilty, Ted K., *The Readability of Numerical Quantities and Abbreviations*, Western Michigan University Center for Educational Studies, 1979.

- Numerical quantities having 5 or fewer digits
  - Example: *28,309* is counted familiar.
  - *1,000,000* is counted unfamiliar.

- The signs: =, +, -, x, ÷

- Numbers used to express monetary values when they contain three or fewer digits to the left of the decimal point.
  - Example: *$127.00* is counted familiar.
  - *$234.56* is counted familiar.
  - *$1,420.00* is counted unfamiliar.
  - *$34,125.45* is counted unfamiliar.

- Ordinal numbers with one or two digits ending in *-st* and *-nd*
  - Example: *1st* is counted as familiar.
  - *92nd* is counted as familiar.
  - But: *139th* is counted as unfamiliar.
  - *2,003rd* is counted as unfamiliar.

- The abbreviations: *yd., ft., in., gal.*

ii. Count as unfamiliar:

- Time, when written in more than one numeral.
  - Example: *12:15 o'clock* is counted unfamiliar
    (*o'clock* is familiar).

- All Roman numerals.

- All decimals, except when used to express monetary values as above.

- All fractions.

  The words and symbols for percent (%, per cent, and percent) are each counted as one unfamiliar word.

REMINDER: REPETITIONS OF UNFAMILIAR WORDS
- The following are counted as often as they are used:
  Dates, e.g., June 5, 1962, are unfamiliar.
  The unfamiliar words in organizations.
  The unfamiliar words in titles of books, documents, films, etc.
  Abbreviations and acronyms.

- "Unfamiliar" names and places are to be counted unfamiliar *only once* in each sample.

A LIST OF 3,000 WORDS KNOWN BY STUDENTS IN GRADE 4
COMPILED BY EDGAR DALE
(REVISED 1983)

Consider as known words on the list with endings indicated in parentheses and words with the following endings, even though they are not noted in parentheses:

- 's, -s, -es, -ies; -d, -ed, -ied, -ing; -r, -er, -est, -ier, -iest

(For further instructions, see pages 13-15.)

A	ah	anger	arrow	back
able	ahead	angry	arrowhead	backache
aboard	aid	animal	art	background
about	aim	ankle	artist	backtrack
above	air (y)	announce (ment)	as	backward(s)
absent	airline	another	ash	bacon
accept	airplane	answer	aside	bad
accident	airport	ant	ask	badge
account	alarm	any	asleep	bag
ache	album	anybody	astronaut	baggage
acid	alike	anyhow	at	bait
acorn	alive	anyone	ate	bake
across	all	anything	atlas	bakery
act	alley	anyway	attack	balance
action	alligator	anywhere	attend	ball
add	all right	apart	attention	balloon
addition	almost	apartment	August	ballpoint
address	alone	ape	aunt	banana
adjust (ment)	along	apiece	author	band
admire	alongside	appear	auto	bandage
admission	aloud	applause	automobile	bang
adore	alphabet	apple	autumn	banjo
adult	already	April	avenue	bank
adventure	also	apron	awake (n)	bar
advice	always	are (n't)	award	barbecue (sauce)
afraid	am	area (place)	away	barber
after	A.M.	arise	awful	bare
afternoon	amaze (ment)	arithmetic	awhile	barefoot
afterward (s)	America (n)	arm	ax(e)	bark
again	among	army		barn
against	amount	around	**B**	barrel
age	an	arrange	baa	base
ago	and	arrest	baby	baseball
agree	angel	arrive	baby-sitter	basement

basket	beneath	bloom	brand	bunny
basketball	berry	blossom	brand-new	burglar
bat	beside(s)	blot	brass	burn (t)
bath (e)	best	blouse	brave (ry)	burro
bathroom	bet	blow	bread	burst
battle	better	blue	break	bury
be	between	blueberry	breakfast	bus
beach	beyond	blush	breast	bush
bead	bib	board	breath (e)	bushel
beak	bible	boat	breeze	business
beam	bicycle	bobwhite	brick	busy
bean	big (ness)	body	bride	but
bear	bill	bodyguard	bridge	butcher
beard	billfold	boil	bright (en)	butter
beast	billion	bold	bring	butterfly
beat	billy goat	bolt	broad	butterscotch
beautiful	bingo	bomb	broadcast	button
beauty	bird	bone	broke (n)	buy
beaver	birth	bonnet	broken-hearted	buzz
because	birthday	boo	brook	by
become (came)	biscuit	book	broom	bye
bed	bit	boom	brother	
bedroom	bite	boot	brought	
bedspread	bitter	born	brown	**C**
bee	black (ness)	borrow	brownie	cab
beef	blackboard	boss	brush	cabbage
beefsteak	blacksmith	both	bubble	cabin
been	blame	bother	bucket	cage
beer	blank	bottle	buckle	cake
beet	blanket	bottom	bud	calendar
before	blast	bought	budge	calf
beg	blastoff	boulder	buffalo	call
beggar	blaze	bounce	bug	came
begin (gan) (gun)	bleed	bow	buggy	camel
behave	bless	bowl	build (ing)	camera
behind	blew	bow-wow	bulb	camp
belief	blind	box	bull	can ('t)
believe	blindfold	boxcar	bullet	canal
bell	blink	boy	bulletin board	canary
belly	blinker	brace	bumblebee	candle
belong (ings)	block	bracelet	bump (y)	candy
below	blond (e)	brain	bun	cane
belt	blood	brake	bunch	cannon
bench	bloodhound	bran	bundle	cannot
bend (t)	bloodstream	branch	bunk	canoe
				canyon

cap	champion	Christmas	college	coward
cape	chance	church	color (ful)	cowboy
capital	change	churn	colt	cozy (sy)
capsule	channel (TV)	cigarette	column	crab
captain	chapter	circle	comb	crack
capture	charge	circus	come	cracker
car	charm	citizen	comfort (able)	cradle
card	chart	city	comic	cranberry
cardboard	chase	clap	comma	crank
care	chatter	class	command	crash
careful (ly)	cheap	classroom	commercial	crawl
careless	cheat	claw	company	crayon
carload	check	clay	complete	crazy
carpenter	checkers	clean	computer	cream (y)
carpet	checkup	cleanser	concrete	creature
carriage	cheek	clear	conductor	creek
carrot	cheer (ful) (ly)	clerk	cone	creep
carry	cheese	clever	connect	crib
cart	cheeseburger	click	contest	cricket
cartoon	cherry	climate	continue	crime
carve	chest	climb	control	cripple
case	chestnut	clip	cook	crisp
cash	chew	clock	cooky (ie)	croak
cashier	chick	close	cool	crook
cash register	chicken	closet	copy	crop
castle	chief	cloth	cord	cross
cat	child (ren)	cloud (y)	cork	crosswalk
catch	childhood	clown	corn	crossways
caterpillar	chili	club	corner	crow
catsup	chill (y)	clubhouse	cornmeal	crowd
cattle	chimney	coach	correct	crown
caught	chimpanzee	coal	cost	cruel
cause	chin	coast	cottage	crumb
cave	china	Coast Guard	cotton	crumble
ceiling	chip	coat	couch	crush
celebrate (ion)	chipmunk	cob	cough	crutch
cell	chirp	cobweb	could (n't)	crust
cellar	chocolate	cocktail	count	cry
cent	choice	cocoa	counter	cub
center	choke	coconut	country	cup (ful)
cereal	choose	coffee	course	cupboard
certain	chop	coin	court	cure
chain	chop suey	cold	cousin	curl (y)
chair	chorus	collar	cover	curtain
chalk (board)	chose (n)	collect (ion) (or)	cow	curve

cushion

customer

cut

cute

D

dad (dy)

daddy-long-legs

daily

dairy

daisy

dam

damage

damp

dance

dandy

danger (ous)

dare

dark (ness)

darling

dart

dash

date

daughter

dawn

day

daylight

daytime

dead

deaf

deal

dear

death

December

decide

deck

deep

deer

defend

delighted

deliver (y)

den

dentist

depend

deposit

describe

desert

design

desire

desk

destroy

detective

detergent

devil

dew

dial

diamond

dice

dictionary

did (n't)

die

diet

difference (ent)

difficult (y)

dig

dim

dime

dimple

dine

ding-dong

dinner

dinosaur

dip

direct

direction

dirt (y)

disagree

disappear

discover

disease

disgrace (ful)

dish

dismiss

distance

ditch

dive

divide

do

dock

doctor

dodge

does (n't)

dog

doll (y)

dollar

done

donkey

don't

door

doorstep

dope

dot

double

dove

down

downstairs

downtown

downward (s)

dozen

drag

dragon

drain

drank

draw

dream

dress

drew

drill

drink

drip

drive

driveway

drop

drove

drown

drowsy

drug

drugstore

drum

drunk

dry

duck (ling)

due

dug

dull

dumb

dump

during

dust (y)

dying

E

each

eager

eagle

ear

earache

eardrum

early

earn (ings)

earth

earthquake

east (ern)

Easter

easy

eat (en)

edge

education

egg

eight

eighteen

eighth

eighty

either

elastic

elbow

election

electric

electricity

elephant

elevator

eleven

elf

elm

else

empty

encyclopedia

end

endless

enemy

engine

engineer

English

enjoy (ment)

enough

enter

envelope

equal

equator

erase

errand

escape

Eskimo

evaporate

even

evening

ever

everlasting

every

everybody

everyday

everyone

everything

everywhere

evil

exactly

example

excellent

except

exchange

excited

exciting

excuse

exercise

exit

expect

experiment

explain

explode

explore

explosive

express (way)

extra

eye

eyeball

eyebrow	feet	flap	fort	gangster
eyeglass	fell	flare	fortune	garage
eyelash	fellow	flash	forty	garbage
eyelid	felt	flashlight	forward	garden
eyesight	female	flat	fought	gargle
	fence	flavor	found	gas
F	fern	flea	fountain	gasoline
fable	festival	flesh	four	gate
face	fever	flew	fourteen	gather
fact	few	flies	fourth	gauge
factory	fib	flight	fox	gave
fade	fiddle	flip	frame	gay
fail (ure)	field	float	freckles	geese
faint	fifteen	flock	free	general
fair	fifth	flood	freedom	gentle
fairy (land)	fifty	floor	freeze	gentleman (men)
faith	fig	flour	freight	geography
fake	fight	flow	fresh	get
fall	figure	flower	Friday	ghost
false	file	flu	friend	giant
family	fill	flunk	friendship	gift
fan	film	flute	frighten	giggle
fancy	final	fly	frog	gill
far	finally	foam	from	giraffe
faraway	find	fog (gy)	front	girl
fare	fine	fold	frost	give (n)
farm	finger (nail) (tip)	folks	frown	glad (ness)
farmer	fingerprint	follow	froze	glance
far-off	finish	fond	fruit	glare
farther	fire	food	fry	glass
fashion	fireplace	fool (ish)	fudge	glassware
fast	fire extinguisher	foot	fuel	glide
fasten	firefly	football	full	globe
fat	fire plug	footpath	fun	glory
father	fireproof	footprint	funny	glove
fault	fireworks	footsteps	fur	glow
favor	first	for	furniture	glue
favorite	fish	force	further	go
fear	fist	forehead		goal
feast	fit	forest	**G**	goat
feather	five	forever	gallon	gobble
February	fix	forget (ful)	gallop	God (g)
fed	fizz	forgot (ten)	gamble	godmother
feed	flag	fork	game	gold (en)
feel	flame	form	gang	goldfish

golf	grip	hard	hide	hop
gone	grizzly	hardware	hide-and-seek	hope
good	groan	harm (less) (ful)	hideout	hopscotch
good-by (bye)	grocery	harness	hi-fi	horn
goodies	groom	harp	high	horse
goodness	ground	harvest	high school	hose
goose	group	has (n't)	highway	hospital
got (gotten)	grow (n)	hat	hike	hot
government	growl	hatch	hill (y)	hot dog
governor	grown-up	hatchet	him	hotel
gown	growth	hate	himself	hound
grab	guard	haul	hint	hour
grace	guess	have (n't)	hip	house
grade	guest	hawk	hippo	housekeeper
grain	guide	hay	hire	housewife
grand	guitar	he	his	how
grandchild	gum	head	history	howl
granddaughter	gun	headache	hit	hug
grandfather	guy	headline	hitch	huge
grandma	gym	headquarters	hive	hum
grandmother		heal	ho	human
grandpa	**H**	health (y)	hobble	hump
grandson	habit	heap	hobby	hundred
grandstand	had (n't)	hear	hockey	hung
grape	hail	heard	hoe	hunger
grapefruit	hair (y)	heart	hold	hungry
grass	half	heat	holdup	hunk
grasshopper	hall	heaven	hole	hunt
grave	Halloween	heavy	holiday	hurricane
gravel	hallway	heel	hollow	hurry
graveyard	ham	height	holster	hurt
gravy	hamburger	held	holy	husband
gray (grey)	hammer	helicopter	home	hush
graze	hamster	hell	home run	hut
grease (y)	hand (ful)	he'll	homesick	hymn
great	handkerchief	hello	homework	
greedy	handle	helmet	honest	**I**
green	handmade	help (ful)	honey	I
greens	handsome	hen	honeybee	ice (y)
greet	handwriting	her	honk	iceberg
grew	hang	herd	honor	ice cream
greyhound	happen	here	hood	I'd
grill	happiness	hero	hoof	idea
grin	happy	herself	hook	if
grind	harbor	hid (den)	hoot	igloo

ill
I'll
I'm
imagine
important
impossible
improve
in
inch
indeed
Indian
indoors
industry
ink
inn
insect
inside
inspection
instead
intend
interest
into
introduce
invent (or)
invite
iron
is (n't)
island
It ('ll) ('s)
I've
ivory
ivy

J
jack
jack-o-lantern
jacket
jackpot
jacks
jail
jam
janitor
January
jar
jaw

jawbone
jay
jaywalker
jazz
jeans
jeep
jelly
jerk
jet
jewel (ry)
jig
job
join
joke
jolly
journey
joy (ful)
judge
jug
juice (y)
July
jump
June
jungle
junk
just

K
kangaroo
ketchup
keep (kept)
kettle
key
kick
kid
kidnap
kill
kind (ness)
kindergarten
king
kiss
kit
kitchen
kite
kitten

kitty
knee
kneel
knew
knife (ves)
knight
knit
knob
knock
knot
know (n)

L
lace
lad
ladder
lady
laid
lake
lamb
lame
lamp
land
lane
language
lantern
lap
large
last
late
laugh
laundry
law
lawn
lawyer
lay
lazy
lead
leaf (ves)
leak
lean
leap
learn
leather
leave

led
left
leg
lemon (ade)
lend
length
lens
leopard
less
lesson
let
letter
lettuce
level
liar
liberty
librarian
library
lick
lid
lie
life
lifeboat
lifeguard
life preserver
lift
light (ness)
lighthouse
lightning
like
lily
limb
lime
Lincoln, Abraham
line
linen
lion
lip
lipstick
liquor
list
listen
litterbug
little
live

liver
lizard
load
loaf (ves)
loan
lobster
lock
log
lollipop
London
lone
lonesome
long
look
loop
loose
lord (L)
lose
loss
lost
lot
lotion
loud
loudspeaker
love
low
luck (y)
luggage
lullaby
lumber
lump
lunch
lung
luxury
lying

M
ma
macaroni
machine
mad
made
magazine
magic
magnet

maid	melon	misplace	Mr.	neighborhood
mail	melt	misprint	Mrs.	neither
mailman	member	miss (M)	much	nerve
major	memorize	missile	mud	nest
majorette	memory	misspell	muffin	net
make	men	mist (y)	mule	never
make-believe	mend	mistake	multiply	new
male	mention	mister	multiplication	newborn
mama	menu	mitt	mumps	newcomer
man	meow	mitten	murder	news
manage	merchant	mix	museum	newscast
manager	mermaid	mixture	mush	newspaper
mane	merry	mob	mushroom	next
manners	merry-go-round	model	music	nibble
many	mess	modern	musical	nice
map	message	moist	musician	nickel
maple	messenger	moisture	must (n't)	nickname
marble	met	mom	mustard	night
march	metal	moment	my	nightfall
March	meter	Monday	myself	nightmare
mark	mice	money	mystery	nighttime
market	microphone	monkey		nine
marriage	middle	monster	**N**	nineteen
marry	midget	month	nail	ninety
marvelous	midnight	moo	name	ninth
mash	midsummer	moon	nap	nipple
mask	might (y)	moonlight	napkin	no
master	mile	moose	narrow	nobody
match	milk	mop	nasty	nod
mate	milkshake	more	nation	noise (y)
matter	mill	morning	nature	none
mattress	million	most	naughty	noodle
may	millionaire	motel	navy	noon
May	mind	moth	near	normal
maybe	mine	mother	nearby	north (ern)
mayor	miner	motion	neat	nose
me	minister	motor	neatness	not
meadow	mink	motorcycle	necessary	note
meal	minnow	mountain	neck	nothing
mean	mint	mouse	necklace	notice
meaning	minute	mouth	necktie	November
measure	miracle	movable	need (n't)	now
meat	mirror	move (able)	needle	nowhere
medicine	misery	movie	Negro	number
meet	mislay	mow	neighbor	nurse

nursery	ostrich	pancake	people	pity
nut	other	panda	pep (py)	pizza
	ouch	pants	pepper	place
O	ought	papa	peppermint	plain
oak	ounce	paper	perfume	plan
oar	our	parade	perhaps	plane
oatmeal	ourselves	pardon	period	planet
oats	out (er)	parent	permit	plant
obey	outdoors	park	person	plantation
ocean	outlaw	parrot	personal	plaster
o'clock	outline	part	pest	plate
October	outside	partner	pet	play (ful)
octopus	oven	partnership	phone	playground
odd	over	party	phonograph	playhouse
of	overalls	pass	photo	playmate
of course	overboard	passenger	photograph	plaything
off	overcoat	password	piano	pleasant
offer	overdo (done)	past	pick	please
office	overeat	paste	pickle	pleasure
often	overflow	pasture	picnic	plenty
oh	overhead	pat	picture	plow
oil	overnight	patch	pie	plug
O.K.	overseas	path	piece	plum
okay	overtime	pave	pig	plumber
old	overweight	paw	pigeon	plus
on	owe	pay	pile	P.M.
once	owl	payment	Pilgrim	pocket
one	own	pea	pill	pocketbook
one-fourth		peace (ful)	pillow	poem
oneself	**P**	peach	pilot	point
one-way	Pa	peacock	pimple	poison
onion	pack	peak	pin	poke
only	package	peanut	pine	pole
onward (s)	pad	pear	pineapple	police (man)
open	page	pearl	ping-pong	polite
operator	paid	pecan	pingpong	pond
opossum	pail	peck	pink	pony
or	pain (ful)	peek	pint	poodle
orange	paint	peel	pioneer	pool
orbit	pair	peep	pipe	poor
orchard	pajamas	peg	pistol	pop
order	pal	pen	pit	popcorn
ordinary	palace	pencil	pitch	poppy
organ	pale	penguin	pitcher	porch
orphan	pan	penny	pitiful	pork

pose

possible

post

postage

postman

postmark

post office

postpone

pot

potato (es)

potato chip

pottery

pound

pour

powder

power (ful)

prairie

praise

pray (er)

prepare

present

President (p)

press

pretend

pretty

prevent

price

primary

prince

princess

print

prison

private

prize

problem

program

promise

promote

proof

property

protect

proud

prove

prune

public

puddle

puff

pull

pump

pumpkin

punch

punish

pup (py)

pupil

puppet

pure

purple

purse

push

puss (y)

put

puzzle

Q

quack (duck)

quarrel

quart

quarter

quarterback

queen

queer

question

quick (ly)

quiet

quilt

quit

quite

R

rabbit

raccoon

race

rack

radio

radish

rag

rail

railroad

rain (y)

rainbow

raindrop

raise

raisin

rake

ram

ran

ranch

rang

range

rap

rascal

rat

rate

rather

rattle

rattlesnake

raw

ray

rayon

razor

reach

read

ready

real

really

rear

reason

rebuild

receive

recess

record

red

redbird

redbreast

reflect

refresh (ment)

refrigerator

refuse

reindeer

rejoice

rejoin

related

religion

remain

remember

remind

remove

rent

repair

repay

repeat

report

respect

rest

restaurant

rest room

retire

return

review

reward

rhyme

rib

ribbon

rice

rich

rid

riddle

ride

right

rim

ring

rip

ripe

rise

river

road

roar

roast

rob

robber (y)

robe

robin

rock (y)

rocket

rode

roll

roller skate

romance

roof

room

rooster

root

rope

rose

rot

rotten

rough

round

route

row

rowboat

royal

rub

rubber

rug

rule

run

rung

rush

rust (y)

S

sack

sad (ness)

saddle

safe

safety

said

sail (or)

sailboat

saint

salad

sale

salt

same

sample

sand (y)

sandwich

sang

sank

sap

sat

satisfactory

Saturday

sauce

saucer	self, selves	shore	skirt	soda
sausage	selfish	short (ness)	skunk	sofa
save	sell	shot	sky	soft
savings	send (t)	should (n't)	skyscraper	softball
saw	sense	shoulder	slam	soil
sawdust	sensible	shout	slap	sold
say	sentence	shove	slave	soldier
scab	separate	shovel	sled	solid
scale	September	show (n)	sleep (y)	solve
scalp	servant	shower	sleeve	some
scamper	serve	shut	sleigh	somebody
scare (y)	service	shutter	slept	someone
scarecrow	set	shy	slice	something
scarf	settle	sick (ness)	slid	sometime
scatter	seven	side	slide	somewhere
school	seventeen	sidewalk	slim	son
schoolboy	seventh	sigh	slip	song
schoolgirl	seventy	sight	slipper	soon
science	several	sign	slippery	sore
scissors	sew	silence	slosh	sorrow
scoop	shade (y)	silent	slow (ly)	sorry
scooter	shadow	silk	sly	sort
score	shake	sill	small	soul
scout	shall	silly	smart	sound
scrap	shame	silver	smash	soup
scratch	shampoo	simple	smell	sour
scream	shape	sin	smile	south (ern)
screen	share	since	smog	space
screw	sharp	sing	smoke (y)	spaceship
scrub	shave	single	smooth	spade
sea	she ('d) ('ll)	sink	snack	spaghetti
seal	sheep	sip	snail	spank
seam	sheet	sir	snake	spark
search	shelf, shelves	sis	snap	sparrow
seashore	shell	sister	sneeze	speak
season	shepherd	sit	sniff	spear
seat	shine (y)	six	snow (y)	special
second	ship (ment)	sixteen	snowball	speck
secret	shirt	sixth	snowflake	speech
see	shock	sixty	snug	speed
seed	shoe	size	so	speedometer
seem	shoemaker	skate	soak	spell
seen	shook	ski	soap	spend (t)
seesaw	shoot	skin	social	spice
selection	shop	skip	sock	spider

spill	steak	stretch	surprise	taste
spin	steal	strike	surround	tattle
spirit	steam	string	surroundings	tattletale
spit	steel	strip	suspect	tattoo
splash	steep	stripe	swallow	taught
split	steeple	strong	swam	tax
spoil	steer	stuck	swamp	taxpayer
spoke	step	student	swan	tea
sponge	stepfather	studio	swear	teach
spook (y)	stepmother	study	sweat	teacher
spool	stereo	stuff	sweater	team
spoon	stew	stumble	sweep	teapot
sport	stick	stung	sweepstakes	tear
spot	sticky	stunt	sweet (en)	tease
sprain	stiff	style	sweetness	teaspoon
spray	still	subject	sweetheart	teeth
spread	sting	submarine	swell	telegram
spring	stink	subtract	swept	telephone
sprinkle	stir	subtraction	swift	telescope
spy	stitch	such	swim	television
square	stock	suck	swing	tell
squash	stocking	sudden (ly)	switch	temper
squeak (y)	stole (n)	suffer	sword	temperature
squeal	stomach	sugar	syllable	ten
squeeze	stone	suit		tend
squirrel	stood	sum	**T**	tender
stab	stool	summer	table	tennis
stable	stoop	sun (ny)	tablespoon	tent
stack	stop	sunbeam	tablet	tenth
stage	stoplight	sunburn	tack	term
stair	store	Sunday	taffy	terrible
stale	storeroom	sundown	tag	test
stalk	stork	sunflower	tail	than
stamp	storm (y)	sung	tailor	thank (ful)
stand	story	sunk (en)	take (n)	Thanksgiving
star	storyteller	sunlight	tale	that ('s)
starch	stove	sunrise	talk	the
stare	straight (en)	sunset	tall	theater
Stars & Stripes	strange	sunshine	tame	their
start	strap	supper	tan	them
starve	straw	suppose	tangle	then
state	strawberry	sure	tank	there
station	stream	surface	tap	there's
statue	street	surfboard	tape	thermometer
stay	strength	surgeon	tar	these

			U	**V**
they	tiptoe	trap	ugly	vacant
they'd	tire	trash	umbrella	vacation
they'll	tissue	travel	umpire	Valentine
they're	title	tray	uncle	valley
they've	to	treasure	under	valuable
thick	toad	tree	underline	value
thief	toast	trespass	understand	vanish
thin	tobacco	trick	undershirt	varnish
thing	today	tricycle	underwear	vase
think	toe	trim	undress	vegetable
third	together	trip	uneducated	velvet
thirst (y)	toilet	trombone	unemployed	verse
thirteen	told	troop	unfair	very
thirty	tomato	trophy	unfasten	vessel
this	tomorrow	trouble	unfinished	vest
thorn	ton	truck	unfold	vice-president
those	tone	true	unfurnished	view
thought (ful)	tongue	truly	unhappy	village
thoughtless	tonight	trumpet	uniform	vine
thousand	too	trunk	United States	violet
thread	took	trust	unkind	violin
three	tool	truth (ful)	unknown	visit (or)
threw	tooth	try	unnecessary	vitamin
throat	toothbrush	tub	unsafe	voice
throne	toothpaste	tube	untie	volleyball
through	top	Tuesday	until	vote
throw (n)	tore (n)	tug	untrue	
thumb	tornado	tulip	unwilling	**W**
thunder	torpedo	tumble	unwise	waffle
Thursday	tortoise	tune	unwrap	wag
tick	toss	tunnel	up	wagon
tick-tock	total	turkey	upon	waist
ticket	touch	turn	upper	wait
tickle	toward	turnip	upset	waiter
tiddlywinks	towel	turtle	upside down	wake (n)
tie	town	TV	upstairs	walk
tiger	toy	twelve	uptown	wall
tight	trace	twenty	upward	wallet
till	track	twice	us	walnut
timber	tractor	twig	U.S.	wander
time	trade	twin	U.S.A.	want
tin	traffic	twist	use	war
tinkle	trail	two	useful	warm
tiny	train	type	usher	warmth
tip	tramp	typewriter		

warn	weed	whole	woke	wrote
wart	week	whom	wolf, wolves	
was (n't)	weekdays	whooping cough	woman	**X**
wash	weekend	whose	women	Xmas
washer	weep	why	won	X-ray
Washington, D.C.	weigh (t)	wicked	wonder (ful)	
George Washington	welcome	wide	won't	**Y**
washroom	well	wide-awake	wood (en)	yard
wasp	went	wife	woodchuck	yarn
waste	were (n't)	wigwam	woodpecker	yawn
watch	west (ern)	wild	woods	year
watchdog	wet	wildcat	woof	yell
water	whale	wildlife	wool (en)	yellow (ish)
waterfall	what	will	word	yes
watermelon	wheat	willing	wore	yet
waterproof	wheel	willow	work	yesterday
wave	wheelbarrow	win	workman	yolk
wax	when	wind (y)	world	yonder
way	where ('s)	window	worm	you ('d) ('ll)
we ('ll) ('re)	which	windowpane	worn	young
weak (en) (ness)	while	wine	worry	youngster
wealth	whip	wing	worse (t)	your
weapon	whirl	wink	worth	yourself
wear	whirlpool	winter	would (n't)	youth
weather	whirlwind	wipe	wound	
weave	whisker	wire	wrap	**Z**
web	whisper	wise	wreck	zebra
wedding	whistle	wish	wren	zero
Wednesday	white	witch	wrist	zone
wee	whiteness	with	write (ten)	zoo
	who ('s)	without	wrong	

TABLE 2-1 FOR OBTAINING CLOZE SCORES

Number of complete sentences in sample

	1	2	3	4	5	6	7
0	-5.00	29.50	41.00	46.75	50.20	52.50	54.14
1	-5.95	28.55	40.05	45.80	49.25	51.55	53.19
2	-6.90	27.60	39.10	44.85	48.30	50.60	52.24
3	-7.85	26.65	38.15	43.90	47.35	49.65	51.29
4	-8.80	25.70	37.20	42.95	46.40	48.70	50.34
5	-9.75	24.75	36.25	42.00	45.45	47.75	49.39
6	-10.70	23.80	35.30	41.05	44.50	46.80	48.44
7	-11.65	22.85	34.35	40.10	43.55	45.85	47.49
8	-12.60	21.90	33.40	39.15	42.60	44.90	46.54
9	-13.55	20.95	32.45	38.20	41.65	43.95	45.59
10	-14.50	20.00	31.50	37.25	40.70	43.00	44.64
11	-15.45	19.05	30.55	36.30	39.75	42.05	43.69
12	-16.40	18.10	29.60	35.35	38.80	41.10	42.74
13	-17.35	17.15	28.65	34.40	37.85	40.15	41.79
14	-18.30	16.20	27.70	33.45	36.90	39.20	40.84
15	-19.25	15.25	26.75	32.50	35.95	38.25	39.89
16	-20.20	14.30	25.80	31.55	35.00	37.30	38.94
17	-21.15	13.35	24.85	30.60	34.05	36.35	37.99
18	-22.10	12.40	23.90	29.65	33.10	35.40	37.04
19	-23.05	11.45	22.95	28.70	32.15	34.45	36.09
20	-24.00	10.50	22.00	27.75	31.20	33.50	35.14
21	-24.95	9.55	21.05	26.80	30.25	32.55	34.19
22	-25.90	8.60	20.10	25.85	29.30	31.60	33.24
23	-26.85	7.65	19.15	24.90	28.35	30.65	32.29
24	-27.80	6.70	18.20	23.95	27.40	29.70	31.34
25	-28.75	5.75	17.25	23.00	26.45	28.75	30.39
26	-29.70	4.80	16.30	22.05	25.50	27.80	29.44
27	-30.65	3.85	15.35	21.10	24.55	26.85	28.49
28	-31.60	2.90	14.40	20.15	23.60	25.90	27.54
29	-32.55	1.95	13.45	19.20	22.65	24.95	26.59
30	-33.50	1.00	12.50	18.25	21.70	24.00	25.64
31	-34.45	0.05	11.55	17.30	20.75	23.05	24.69
32	-35.40	-0.90	10.60	16.35	19.80	22.10	23.74
33	-36.35	-1.85	9.65	15.40	18.85	21.15	22.79
34	-37.30	-2.80	8.70	14.45	17.90	20.20	21.84
35	-38.25	-3.75	7.75	13.50	16.95	19.25	20.89
36	-39.20	-4.70	6.80	12.55	16.00	18.30	19.94
37	-40.15	-5.65	5.85	11.60	15.05	17.35	18.99
38	-41.10	-6.60	4.90	10.65	14.10	16.40	18.04
39	-42.05	-7.55	3.95	9.70	13.15	15.45	17.09
40	-43.00	-8.50	3.00	8.75	12.20	14.50	16.14
41	-43.95	-9.45	2.05	7.80	11.25	13.55	15.19
42	-44.90	-10.40	1.10	6.85	10.30	12.60	14.24
43	-45.85	-11.35	0.15	5.90	9.35	11.65	13.29
44	-46.80	-12.30	-0.80	4.95	8.40	10.70	12.34
45	-47.75	-13.25	-1.75	4.00	7.45	9.75	11.39
46	-48.70	-14.20	-2.70	3.05	6.50	8.80	10.44
47	-49.65	-15.15	-3.65	2.10	5.55	7.85	9.49
48	-50.60	-16.10	-4.60	1.15	4.60	6.90	8.54
49	-51.55	-17.05	-5.55	0.20	3.65	5.95	7.59
50	-52.50	-18.00	-6.50	-0.75	2.70	5.00	6.64

Number of unfamiliar words in sample

TABLE 2-1 CONTINUED

Number of complete sentences in sample

	8	9	10	11	12	13	14
0	55.38	56.33	57.10	57.73	58.25	58.69	59.07
1	54.42	55.38	56.15	56.78	57.30	57.74	58.12
2	53.47	54.43	55.20	55.83	56.35	56.79	57.17
3	52.52	53.48	54.25	54.88	55.40	55.84	56.22
4	51.57	52.53	53.30	53.93	54.45	54.89	55.27
5	50.63	51.58	52.35	52.98	53.50	53.94	54.32
6	49.67	50.63	51.40	52.03	52.55	52.99	53.37
7	48.72	49.68	50.45	51.08	51.60	52.04	52.42
8	47.77	48.73	49.50	50.13	50.65	51.09	51.47
9	46.82	47.78	48.55	49.18	49.70	50.14	50.52
10	45.88	46.83	47.60	48.23	48.75	49.19	49.57
11	44.92	45.88	46.65	47.28	47.80	48.24	48.62
12	43.97	44.93	45.70	46.33	46.85	47.29	47.67
13	43.02	43.98	44.75	45.38	45.90	46.34	46.72
14	42.07	43.03	43.80	44.43	44.95	45.39	45.77
15	41.13	42.08	42.85	43.48	44.00	44.44	44.82
16	40.17	41.13	41.90	42.53	43.05	43.49	43.87
17	39.23	40.18	40.95	41.58	42.10	42.54	42.92
18	38.28	39.23	40.00	40.63	41.15	41.59	41.97
19	37.33	38.28	39.05	39.68	40.20	40.64	41.02
20	36.38	37.33	38.10	38.73	39.25	39.69	40.07
21	35.43	36.38	37.15	37.78	38.30	38.74	39.12
22	34.48	35.43	36.20	36.83	37.35	37.79	38.17
23	33.53	34.48	35.25	35.88	36.40	36.84	37.22
24	32.58	33.53	34.30	34.93	35.45	35.89	36.27
25	31.63	32.58	33.35	33.98	34.50	34.94	35.32
26	30.68	31.63	32.40	33.03	33.55	33.99	34.37
27	29.73	30.68	31.45	32.08	32.60	33.04	33.42
28	28.78	29.73	30.50	31.13	31.65	32.09	32.47
29	27.83	28.78	29.55	30.18	30.70	31.14	31.52
30	26.88	27.83	28.60	29.23	29.75	30.19	30.57
31	25.93	26.88	27.65	28.28	28.80	29.24	29.62
32	24.98	25.93	26.70	27.33	27.85	28.29	28.67
33	24.03	24.98	25.75	26.38	26.90	27.34	27.72
34	23.08	24.03	24.80	25.43	25.95	26.39	26.77
35	22.13	23.08	23.85	24.48	25.00	25.44	25.82
36	21.18	22.13	22.90	23.53	24.05	24.49	24.87
37	20.23	21.18	21.95	22.58	23.10	23.54	23.92
38	19.28	20.23	21.00	21.63	22.15	22.59	22.97
39	18.33	19.28	20.05	20.68	21.20	21.64	22.02
40	17.38	18.33	19.10	19.73	20.25	20.69	21.07
41	16.43	17.38	18.15	18.78	19.30	19.74	20.12
42	15.48	16.43	17.20	17.83	18.35	18.79	19.17
43	14.53	15.48	16.25	16.88	17.40	17.84	18.22
44	13.58	14.53	15.30	15.93	16.45	16.89	17.27
45	12.63	13.58	14.35	14.98	15.50	15.94	16.32
46	11.68	12.63	13.40	14.03	14.55	14.99	15.37
47	10.73	11.68	12.45	13.08	13.60	14.04	14.42
48	9.78	10.73	11.50	12.13	12.65	13.09	13.47
49	8.83	9.78	10.55	11.18	11.70	12.14	12.52
50	7.88	8.83	9.60	10.23	10.75	11.19	11.57

Number of unfamiliar words sample

TABLE 2-1 CONTINUED

Number of complete sentences in sample

	15	16	17	18	19	20	21
0	59.40	59.69	59.94	60.17	60.37	60.55	60.71
1	58.45	58.74	58.99	59.22	59.42	59.60	59.76
2	57.50	57.79	58.04	58.27	58.47	58.65	58.81
3	56.55	56.84	57.09	57.32	57.52	57.70	57.86
4	55.60	55.89	56.14	56.37	56.57	56.75	56.91
5	54.65	54.94	55.19	55.42	55.62	55.80	55.96
6	53.70	53.99	54.24	54.47	54.67	54.85	55.01
7	52.75	53.04	53.29	53.52	53.72	53.90	54.06
8	51.80	52.09	52.34	52.57	52.77	52.95	53.11
9	50.85	51.14	51.39	51.62	51.82	52.00	52.16
10	49.90	50.19	50.44	50.67	50.87	51.05	51.21
11	48.95	49.24	49.49	49.72	49.92	50.10	50.26
12	48.00	48.29	48.54	48.77	48.97	49.15	49.31
13	47.05	47.34	47.59	47.82	48.02	48.20	48.36
14	46.10	46.39	46.64	46.87	47.07	47.25	47.41
15	45.15	45.44	45.69	45.92	46.12	46.30	46.46
16	44.20	44.49	44.74	44.97	45.17	45.35	45.51
17	43.25	43.54	43.79	44.02	44.22	44.40	44.56
18	42.30	42.59	42.84	43.07	43.27	43.45	43.61
19	41.35	41.64	41.89	42.12	42.32	42.50	42.66
20	40.40	40.69	40.94	41.17	41.37	41.55	41.71
21	39.45	39.74	39.99	40.22	40.42	40.60	40.76
22	38.50	38.79	39.04	39.27	39.47	39.65	39.81
23	37.55	37.84	38.09	38.32	38.52	38.70	38.86
24	36.60	36.89	37.14	37.37	37.57	37.75	37.91
25	35.65	35.94	36.19	36.42	36.62	36.80	36.96
26	34.70	34.99	35.24	35.47	35.67	35.85	36.01
27	33.75	34.04	34.29	34.52	34.72	34.90	35.06
28	32.80	33.09	33.34	33.57	33.77	33.95	34.11
29	31.85	32.14	32.39	32.62	32.82	33.00	33.16
30	30.90	31.19	31.44	31.67	31.87	32.05	32.21
31	29.95	30.24	30.49	30.72	30.92	31.10	31.26
32	29.00	29.29	29.54	29.77	29.97	30.15	30.31
33	28.05	28.34	28.59	28.82	29.02	29.20	29.36
34	27.10	27.39	27.64	27.87	28.07	28.25	28.41
35	26.15	26.44	26.69	26.92	27.12	27.30	27.46
36	25.20	25.49	25.74	25.97	26.17	26.35	26.51
37	24.25	24.54	24.79	25.02	25.22	25.40	25.56
38	23.30	23.59	23.84	24.07	24.27	24.45	24.61
39	22.35	22.64	22.89	23.12	23.32	23.50	23.66
40	21.40	21.69	21.94	22.17	22.37	22.55	22.71
41	20.45	20.74	20.99	21.22	21.42	21.60	21.76
42	19.50	19.79	20.04	20.27	20.47	20.65	20.81
43	18.55	18.84	19.09	19.32	19.52	19.70	19.86
44	17.60	17.89	18.14	18.37	18.57	18.75	18.91
45	16.65	16.94	17.19	17.42	17.62	17.80	17.96
46	15.70	15.99	16.24	16.47	16.67	16.85	17.01
47	14.75	15.04	15.29	15.52	15.72	15.90	16.06
48	13.80	14.09	14.34	14.57	14.77	14.95	15.11
49	12.85	13.14	13.39	13.62	13.82	14.00	14.16
50	11.90	12.19	12.44	12.67	12.87	13.05	13.21

Number of unfamiliar words in sample

TABLE 2-1 CONTINUED

Number of complete sentences in sample

	22	23	24	25	26	27	28
0	60.86	61.00	61.13	61.24	61.35	61.44	61.54
1	59.91	60.05	60.17	60.29	60.40	60.49	60.59
2	58.96	59.10	59.22	59.34	59.45	59.54	59.64
3	58.01	58.15	58.27	58.39	58.50	58.59	58.69
4	57.06	57.20	57.32	57.44	57.55	57.64	57.74
5	56.11	56.25	56.38	56.49	56.60	56.69	56.79
6	55.16	55.30	55.42	55.54	55.65	55.74	55.84
7	54.21	54.35	54.47	54.59	54.70	54.79	54.89
8	53.26	53.40	53.52	53.64	53.75	53.84	53.94
9	52.31	52.45	52.57	52.69	52.80	52.89	52.99
10	51.36	51.50	51.63	51.74	51.85	51.94	52.04
11	50.41	50.55	50.67	50.79	50.90	50.99	51.09
12	49.46	49.60	49.72	49.84	49.95	50.04	50.14
13	48.51	48.65	48.77	48.89	49.00	49.09	49.19
14	47.56	47.70	47.82	47.94	48.05	48.14	48.24
15	46.61	46.75	46.88	46.99	47.10	47.19	47.29
16	45.66	45.80	45.92	46.04	46.15	46.24	46.34
17	44.71	44.85	44.98	45.09	45.20	45.29	45.39
18	43.76	43.90	44.03	44.14	44.25	44.34	44.44
19	42.81	42.95	43.08	43.19	43.30	43.39	43.49
20	41.86	42.00	42.13	42.24	42.35	42.44	42.54
21	40.91	41.05	41.18	41.29	41.40	41.49	41.59
22	39.96	40.10	40.23	40.34	40.45	40.54	40.64
23	39.01	39.15	39.28	39.39	39.50	39.59	39.69
24	38.06	38.20	38.33	38.44	38.55	38.64	38.74
25	37.11	37.25	37.38	37.49	37.60	37.69	37.79
26	36.16	36.30	36.43	36.54	36.65	36.74	36.84
27	35.21	35.35	35.48	35.59	35.70	35.79	35.89
28	34.26	34.40	34.53	34.64	34.75	34.84	34.94
29	33.31	33.45	33.58	33.69	33.80	33.89	33.99
30	32.36	32.50	32.63	32.74	32.85	32.94	33.04
31	31.41	31.55	31.68	31.79	31.90	31.99	32.09
32	30.46	30.60	30.73	30.84	30.95	31.04	31.14
33	29.51	29.65	29.78	29.89	30.00	30.09	30.19
34	28.56	28.70	28.83	28.94	29.05	29.14	29.24
35	27.61	27.75	27.88	27.99	28.10	28.19	28.29
36	26.66	26.80	26.93	27.04	27.15	27.24	27.34
37	25.71	25.85	25.98	26.09	26.20	26.29	26.39
38	24.76	24.90	25.03	25.14	25.25	25.34	25.44
39	23.81	23.95	24.08	24.19	24.30	24.39	24.49
40	22.86	23.00	23.13	23.24	23.35	23.44	23.54
41	21.91	22.05	22.18	22.29	22.40	22.49	22.59
42	20.96	21.10	21.23	21.34	21.45	21.54	21.64
43	20.01	20.15	20.28	20.39	20.50	20.59	20.69
44	19.06	19.20	19.33	19.44	19.55	19.64	19.74
45	18.11	18.25	18.38	18.49	18.60	18.69	18.79
46	17.16	17.30	17.43	17.54	17.65	17.74	17.84
47	16.21	16.35	16.48	16.59	16.70	16.79	16.89
48	15.26	15.40	15.53	15.64	15.75	15.84	15.94
49	14.31	14.45	14.58	14.69	14.80	14.89	14.99
50	13.36	13.50	13.63	13.74	13.85	13.94	14.04

Number of unfamiliar words in sample

TABLE 2-1 CONTINUED

Number of complete sentences in sample

		29	30	31	32	33	34	35
	0	61.62	61.70	61.77	61.84	61.91	61.97	62.03
	1	60.67	60.75	60.82	60.89	60.96	61.02	61.08
	2	59.72	59.80	59.87	59.94	60.01	60.07	60.13
	3	58.77	58.85	58.92	58.99	59.06	59.12	59.18
	4	57.82	57.90	57.97	58.04	58.11	58.17	58.23
	5	56.87	56.95	57.02	57.09	57.16	57.22	57.28
	6	55.92	56.00	56.07	56.14	56.21	56.27	56.33
	7	54.97	55.05	55.12	55.19	55.26	55.32	55.38
	8	54.02	54.10	54.17	54.24	54.31	54.37	54.43
	9	53.07	53.15	53.22	53.29	53.36	53.42	53.48
	10	52.12	52.20	52.27	52.34	52.41	52.47	52.53
	11	51.17	51.25	51.32	51.39	51.46	51.52	51. 58
	12	50.22	50.30	50.37	50.44	50.51	50.57	50.63
	13	49.27	49.35	49.42	49.49	49.56	49.62	49.68
	14	48.32	48.40	48.47	48.54	48.61	48.67	48.73
Number of unfamiliar words in sample	15	47.37	47.45	47.52	47.59	47.66	47.72	47.78
	16	46.42	46.50	46.57	46.64	46.71	46.77	46.83
	17	45.47	45.55	45.62	45.69	45.76	45.82	45.88
	18	44.52	44.60	44.67	44.74	44.81	44.87	44.93
	19	43.57	43.65	43.72	43.79	43.86	43.92	43.98
	20	42.62	42.70	42.77	42.84	42.91	42.97	43.03
	21	41.67	41.75	41.82	41.89	41.96	42.02	42.08
	22	40.72	40.80	40.87	40.94	41.01	41.07	41.13
	23	39.77	39.85	39.92	39.99	40.06	40.12	40.18
	24	38.82	38.90	38.97	39.04	39.11	39.17	39.23
	25	37.87	37.95	38.02	38.09	38.16	38.22	38.28
	26	36.92	37.00	37.07	37.14	37.21	37.27	37.33
	27	35.97	36.05	36.12	36.19	36.26	36.32	36.38
	28	35.02	35.10	35.17	35.24	35.31	35.37	35.43
	29	34.07	34.15	34.22	34.29	34.36	34.42	34.48
	30	33.12	33.20	33.27	33.34	33.41	33.47	33.53
	31	32.17	32.25	32.32	32.39	32.46	32.52	32.58
	32	31.22	31.30	31.37	31.44	31.51	31.57	31.63
	33	30.27	30.35	30.42	30.49	30.56	30.62	30.68
	34	29.32	29.40	29.47	29.54	29.61	29.67	29.73
	35	28.37	28.45	28.52	28.59	28.66	28.72	28.78
	36	27.42	27.50	27.57	27.64	27.71	27.77	27.83
	37	26.47	26.55	26.62	26.69	26.76	26.82	26.88
	38	25.52	25.60	25.67	25.74	25.81	25.87	25.93
	39	24.57	24.65	24.72	24.79	24.86	24.92	24.98
	40	23.62	23.70	23.77	23.84	23.91	23.97	24.03
	41	22.67	22.75	22.82	22.89	22.96	23.02	23.08
	42	21.72	21.80	21.87	21.94	22.01	22.07	22.13
	43	20.77	20.85	20.92	20.99	21.06	21.12	21.18
	44	19.82	19.90	19.97	20.04	20.11	20.17	20.23
	45	18.87	18.95	19.02	19.09	19.16	19.22	19.28
	46	17.92	18.00	18.07	18.14	18.21	18.27	18.33
	47	16.97	17.05	17.12	17.19	17.26	17.32	17.38
	48	16.02	16.10	16.17	16.24	16.31	16.37	16.43
	49	15.07	15.15	15.22	15.29	15.36	15.42	15.48
	50	14.12	14.20	14.27	14.34	14.41	14.47	14.53

TABLE 2-1 CONTINUED

Number of complete sentences in sample

	36	37	38	39	40
0	62.08	62.14	62.18	62.23	62.27
1	61.13	61.19	61.23	61.28	61.32
2	60.18	60.24	60.28	60.33	60.37
3	59.23	59.29	59.33	59.38	59.42
4	58.28	58.34	58.38	58.43	58.47
5	57.33	57.39	57.43	57.48	57.52
6	56.38	56.44	56.48	56.53	56.57
7	55.43	55.49	55.53	55.58	55.62
8	54.48	54.54	54.58	54.63	54.67
9	53.53	53.59	53.63	53.68	53.72
10	52.58	52.64	52.68	52.73	52.77
11	51.63	51.69	51.73	51.78	51.82
12	50.68	50.74	50.78	50.83	50.87
13	49.73	49.79	49.83	49.88	49.92
14	48.78	48.84	48.88	48.93	48.97
15	47.83	47.89	47.93	47.98	48.02
16	46.88	46.94	46.98	47.03	47.07
17	45.93	45.99	46.03	46.08	46.13
18	44.98	45.04	45.08	45.13	45.18
19	44.03	44.09	44.13	44.18	44.23
20	43.08	43.14	43.18	43.23	43.28
21	42.13	42.19	42.23	42.28	42.32
22	41.18	41.24	41.28	41.33	41.38
23	40.23	40.29	40.33	40.38	40.43
24	39.28	39.34	39.38	39.43	39.48
25	38.33	38.39	38.43	38.48	38.53
26	37.38	37.44	37.48	37.53	37.57
27	36.43	36.49	36.53	36.58	36.63
28	35.48	35.54	35.58	35.63	35.68
29	34.53	34.59	34.63	34.68	34.73
30	33.58	33.64	33.68	33.73	33.78
31	32.63	32.69	32.73	32.78	32.82
32	31.68	31.74	31.78	31.83	31.88
33	30.73	30.79	30.83	30.88	30.93
34	29.78	29.84	29.88	29.93	29.98
35	28.83	28.89	28.93	28.98	29.03
36	27.88	27.94	27.98	28.03	28.07
37	26.93	26.99	27.03	27.08	27.13
38	25.98	26.04	26.08	26.13	26.18
39	25.03	25.09	25.13	25.18	25.23
40	24.08	24.14	24.18	24.23	24.28
41	23.13	23.19	23.23	23.28	23.32
42	22.18	22.24	22.28	22.33	22.38
43	21.23	21.29	21.33	21.38	21.43
44	20.28	20.34	20.38	20.43	20.48
45	19.33	19.39	19.43	19.48	19.53
46	18.38	18.44	18.48	18.53	18.57
47	17.43	17.49	17.53	17.58	17.63
48	16.48	16.54	16.58	16.63	16.68
49	15.53	15.59	15.63	15.68	15.73
50	14.58	14.64	14.68	14.73	14.78

Number of unfamiliar words in sample

TABLE 2-1 CONTINUED

Number of complete sentences in sample

	41	42	43	44	45
0	62.32	62.36	62.40	62.43	62.47
1	61.37	61.41	61.45	61.48	61.52
2	60.42	60.46	60.50	60.53	60.57
3	59.47	59.51	59.55	59.58	59.62
4	58.52	58.56	58.60	58.63	58.67
5	57.57	57.61	57.65	57.68	57.72
6	56.62	56.66	56.70	56.73	56.77
7	55.67	55.71	55.75	55.78	55.82
8	54.72	54.76	54.80	54.83	54.87
9	53.77	53.81	53.85	53.88	53.92
10	52.82	52.86	52.90	52.93	52.97
11	51.87	51.91	51.95	51.98	52.02
12	50.92	50.96	51.00	51.03	51.07
13	49.97	50.01	50.05	50.08	50.12
14	49.02	49.06	49.10	49.13	49.17
15	48.07	48.11	48.15	48.18	48.22
16	47.12	47.16	47.20	47.23	47.27
17	46.17	46.21	46.25	46.28	46.32
18	45.22	45.26	45.30	45.33	45.37
19	44.27	44.31	44.35	44.38	44.42
20	43.32	43.36	43.40	43.43	43.47
21	42.37	42.41	42.45	42.48	42.52
22	41.42	41.46	41.50	41.53	41.57
23	40.47	40.51	40.55	40.58	40.62
24	39.52	39.56	39.60	39.63	39.67
25	38.57	38.61	38.65	38.68	38.72
26	37.62	37.66	37.70	37.73	37.77
27	36.67	36.71	36.75	36.78	36.82
28	35.72	35.76	35.80	35.83	35.87
29	34.77	34.81	34.85	34.88	34.92
30	33.82	33.86	33.90	33.93	33.97
31	32.87	32.91	32.95	32.98	33.02
32	31.92	31.96	32.00	32.03	32.07
33	30.97	31.01	31.05	31.08	31.12
34	30.02	30.16	30.10	30.13	30.17
35	29.07	29.11	29.15	29.18	29.22
36	28.12	28.16	28.20	28.23	28.27
37	27.17	27.21	27.25	27.28	27.32
38	26.22	26.26	26.30	26.33	26.37
39	25.27	25.31	25.35	25.38	25.42
40	24.32	24.36	24.40	24.43	24.47
41	23.37	23.41	23.45	23.48	23.52
42	22.42	22.46	22.50	22.53	22.57
43	21.47	21.51	21.55	21.58	21.62
44	20.52	20.56	20.60	20.63	20.67
45	19.57	19.61	19.65	19.68	19.72
46	18.62	18.66	18.70	18.73	18.77
47	17.67	17.71	17.75	17.78	17.82
48	16.72	16.76	16.80	16.83	16.87
49	15.77	15.81	15.85	15.88	15.92
50	14.82	14.86	14.90	14.93	14.97

Number of unfamiliar words in sample

TABLE 2-1 CONTINUED

Number of complete sentences in sample

	46	47	48	49	50
0	62.50	62.53	62.56	62.59	62.62
1	61.55	61.58	61.61	61.64	61.67
2	60.60	60.63	60.66	60.69	60.72
3	59.65	59.68	59.71	59.74	59.77
4	58.70	58.73	58.76	58.79	58.82
5	57.75	57.78	57.81	57.84	57.87
6	56.80	56.83	56.86	56.89	56.92
7	55.85	55.88	55.91	55.94	55.97
8	54.90	54.93	54.96	54.99	55.02
9	53.95	53.98	54.01	54.04	54.07
10	53.00	53.03	53.06	53.09	53.12
11	52.05	52.08	52.11	52.14	52.17
12	51.10	51.13	51.16	51.19	51.22
13	50.15	50.18	50.21	50.24	50.27
14	49.20	49.23	49.26	49.29	49.32
15	48.25	48.28	48.31	48.34	48.37
16	47.30	47.33	47.36	47.39	47.42
17	46.35	46.38	46.41	46.44	46.47
18	45.40	45.43	45.46	45.49	45.52
19	44.45	44.48	44.51	44.54	44.57
20	43.50	43.53	43.56	43.59	43.62
21	42.55	42.58	42.61	42.64	42.67
22	41.60	41.63	41.66	41.69	41.72
23	40.65	40.68	40.71	40.74	40.77
24	39.70	39.73	39.76	39.79	39.82
25	38.75	38.78	38.81	38.84	38.87
26	37.80	37.83	37.86	37.89	37.92
27	36.85	36.88	36.91	36.94	36.97
28	35.90	35.93	35.96	35.99	36.02
29	34.95	34.98	35.01	35.04	35.07
30	34.00	34.03	34.06	34.09	34.12
31	33.05	33.08	33.11	33.14	33.17
32	32.10	32.13	32.16	32.19	32.22
33	31.15	31.18	31.21	31.24	31.27
34	30.20	30.23	30.26	30.29	30.32
35	29.25	29.28	29.31	29.34	29.37
36	28.30	28.33	28.36	28.39	28.42
37	27.35	27.38	27.41	27.44	27.47
38	26.40	26.43	26.46	26.49	26.52
39	25.45	25.48	25.51	25.54	25.57
40	24.50	24.53	24.56	24.59	24.62
41	23.55	23.58	23.61	23.64	23.67
42	22.60	22.63	22.66	22.69	22.72
43	21.65	21.68	21.71	21.74	21.77
44	20.70	20.73	20.76	20.79	20.82
45	19.75	19.78	19.81	19.84	19.87
46	18.80	18.83	18.86	18.89	18.92
47	17.85	17.88	17.91	17.94	17.97
48	16.90	16.93	16.96	16.99	17.02
49	15.95	15.98	16.01	16.04	16.07
50	15.00	15.03	15.06	15.09	15.12

Number of unfamiliar words in sample

TABLE 2-2 FOR OBTAINING READING LEVELS

Number of sentences in sample

	1	2	3	4	5	6	7	8
0	16	9-10	5-6	4	3	3	2	2
1	16	9-10	5-6	4	3	3	2	2
2	16	9-10	5-6	4	4	3	3	2
3	16	11-12	7-8	5-6	4	3	3	3
4	16	11-12	7-8	5-6	4	4	3	3
5	16	11-12	7-8	5-6	4	4	3	3
6	16	11-12	7-8	5-6	4	4	4	3
7	16	11-12	7-8	5-6	5-6	4	4	4
8	16	11-12	7-8	5-6	5-6	4	4	4
9	16	13-15	9-10	7-8	5-6	5-6	4	4
10	16	13-15	9-10	7-8	5-6	5-6	4	4
11	16	13-15	9-10	7-8	5-6	5-6	5-6	4
12	16	13-15	9-10	7-8	7-8	5-6	5-6	5-6
13	16	13-15	9-10	7-8	7-8	5-6	5-6	5-6
14	16	13-15	9-10	7-8	7-8	5-6	5-6	5-6
15	16	13-15	11-12	9-10	7-8	7-8	5-6	5-6
16	16	16	11-12	9-10	7-8	7-8	7-8	5-6
17	16	16	11-12	9-10	7-8	7-8	7-8	5-6
18	16	16	11-12	9-10	7-8	7-8	7-8	7-8
19	16	16	11-12	9-10	9-10	7-8	7-8	7-8
20	16	16	11-12	9-10	9-10	7-8	7-8	7-8
21	16	16	11-12	11-12	9-10	9-10	7-8	7-8
22	16	16	13-15	11-12	9-10	9-10	7-8	7-8
23	16	16	13-15	11-12	9-10	9-10	9-10	7-8
24	16	16	13-15	11-12	9-10	9-10	9-10	9-10
25	16	16	13-15	11-12	11-12	9-10	9-10	9-10
26	16	16	13-15	11-12	11-12	9-10	9-10	9-10
27	16	16	13-15	11-12	11-12	11-12	9-10	9-10
28	16	16	16	13-15	11-12	11-12	9-10	9-10
29	16	16	16	13-15	11-12	11-12	11-12	9-10
30	16	16	16	13-15	11-12	11-12	11-12	11-12
31	16	16	16	13-15	13-15	11-12	11-12	11-12
32	16	16	16	13-15	13-15	11-12	11-12	11-12
33	16	16	16	13-15	13-15	11-12	11-12	11-12
34	16	16	16	16	13-15	13-15	11-12	11-12
35	16	16	16	16	13-15	13-15	13-15	11-12
36	16	16	16	16	13-15	13-15	13-15	11-12
37	16	16	16	16	13-15	13-15	13-15	13-15
38	16	16	16	16	16	13-15	13-15	13-15
39	16	16	16	16	16	13-15	13-15	13-15
40	16	16	16	16	16	16	13-15	13-15
41	16	16	16	16	16	16	13-15	13-15
42	16	16	16	16	16	16	16	13-15
43	16	16	16	16	16	16	16	16
44	16	16	16	16	16	16	16	16
45	16	16	16	16	16	16	16	16
46	16	16	16	16	16	16	16	16
47	16	16	16	16	16	16	16	16
48	16	16	16	16	16	16	16	16
49	16	16	16	16	16	16	16	16
50	16	16	16	16	16	16	16	16

Number of unfamiliar words in sample

TABLE 2-2 CONTINUED

Number of sentences in sample

Number of unfamiliar words in sample	9	10	11	12	13	14	15	16
0	1	1	1	1	1	1	1	1
1	2	1	1	1	1	1	1	1
2	2	2	2	1	1	1	1	1
3	2	2	2	2	2	1	1	1
4	3	2	2	2	2	2	2	2
5	3	3	3	2	2	2	2	2
6	3	3	3	3	3	2	2	2
7	3	3	3	3	3	3	3	2
8	4	3	3	3	3	3	3	3
9	4	4	3	3	3	3	3	3
10	4	4	4	4	3	3	3	3
11	4	4	4	4	4	4	4	3
12	4	4	4	4	4	4	4	4
13	5-6	4	4	4	4	4	4	4
14	5-6	5-6	4	4	4	4	4	4
15	5-6	5-6	5-6	5-6	4	4	4	4
16	5-6	5-6	5-6	5-6	5-6	5-6	4	4
17	5-6	5-6	5-6	5-6	5-6	5-6	5-6	5-6
18	5-6	5-6	5-6	5-6	5-6	5-6	5-6	5-6
19	7-8	5-6	5-6	5-6	5-6	5-6	5-6	5-6
20	7-8	7-8	7-8	5-6	5-6	5-6	5-6	5-6
21	7-8	7-8	7-8	7-8	7-8	5-6	5-6	5-6
22	7-8	7-8	7-8	7-8	7-8	7-8	7-8	7-8
23	7-8	7-8	7-8	7-8	7-8	7-8	7-8	7-8
24	7-8	7-8	7-8	7-8	7-8	7-8	7-8	7-8
25	9-10	7-8	7-8	7-8	7-8	7-8	7-8	7-8
26	9-10	9-10	7-8	7-8	7-8	7-8	7-8	7-8
27	9-10	9-10	9-10	9-10	7-8	7-8	7-8	7-8
28	9-10	9-10	9-10	9-10	9-10	9-10	9-10	7-8
29	9-10	9-10	9-10	9-10	9-10	9-10	9-10	9-10
30	9-10	9-10	9-10	9-10	9-10	9-10	9-10	9-10
31	11-12	9-10	9-10	9-10	9-10	9-10	9-10	9-10
32	11-12	11-12	9-10	9-10	9-10	9-10	9-10	9-10
33	11-12	11-12	11-12	11-12	9-10	9-10	9-10	9-10
34	11-12	11-12	11-12	11-12	11-12	11-12	9-10	9-10
35	11-12	11-12	11-12	11-12	11-12	11-12	11-12	11-12
36	11-12	11-12	11-12	11-12	11-12	11-12	11-12	11-12
37	11-12	11-12	11-12	11-12	11-12	11-12	11-12	11-12
38	13-15	13-15	11-12	11-12	11-12	11-12	11-12	11-12
39	13-15	13-15	13-15	11-12	11-12	11-12	11-12	11-12
40	13-15	13-15	13-15	13-15	13-15	11-12	11-12	11-12
41	13-15	13-15	13-15	13-15	13-15	13-15	13-15	13-15
42	13-15	13-15	13-15	13-15	13-15	13-15	13-15	13-15
43	13-15	13-15	13-15	13-15	13-15	13-15	13-15	13-15
44	16	13-15	13-15	13-15	13-15	13-15	13-15	13-15
45	16	16	16	13-15	13-15	13-15	13-15	13-15
46	16	16	16	16	16	13-15	13-15	13-15
47	16	16	16	16	16	16	16	13-15
48	16	16	16	16	16	16	16	16
49	16	16	16	16	16	16	16	16
50	16	16	16	16	16	16	16	16

TABLE 2-2 CONTINUED

Number of sentences in sample

	17	18	19	20	21	22	23	24
0	1	1	1	1	1	1	1	1
1	1	1	1	1	1	1	1	1
2	1	1	1	1	1	1	1	1
3	1	1	1	1	1	1	1	1
4	1	1	1	1	1	1	1	1
5	2	2	2	2	2	1	1	1
6	2	2	2	2	2	2	2	2
7	2	2	2	2	2	2	2	2
8	3	3	3	3	2	2	2	2
9	3	3	3	3	3	3	3	3
10	3	3	3	3	3	3	3	3
11	3	3	3	3	3	3	3	3
12	4	4	4	3	3	3	3	3
13	4	4	4	4	4	4	4	4
14	4	4	4	4	4	4	4	4
15	4	4	4	4	4	4	4	4
16	4	4	4	4	4	4	4	4
17	5-6	4	4	4	4	4	4	4
18	5-6	5-6	5-6	5-6	5-6	5-6	5-6	4
19	5-6	5-6	5-6	5-6	5-6	5-6	5-6	5-6
20	5-6	5-6	5-6	5-6	5-6	5-6	5-6	5-6
21	5-6	5-6	5-6	5-6	5-6	5-6	5-6	5-6
22	5-6	5-6	5-6	5-6	5-6	5-6	5-6	5-6
23	7-8	7-8	7-8	7-8	7-8	5-6	5-6	5-6
24	7-8	7-8	7-8	7-8	7-8	7-8	7-8	7-8
25	7-8	7-8	7-8	7-8	7-8	7-8	7-8	7-8
26	7-8	7-8	7-8	7-8	7-8	7-8	7-8	7-8
27	7-8	7-8	7-8	7-8	7-8	7-8	7-8	7-8
28	7-8	7-8	7-8	7-8	7-8	7-8	7-8	7-8
29	9-10	9-10	9-10	9-10	7-8	7-8	7-8	7-8
30	9-10	9-10	9-10	9-10	9-10	9-10	9-10	9-10
31	9-10	9-10	9-10	9-10	9-10	9-10	9-10	9-10
32	9-10	9-10	9-10	9-10	9-10	9-10	9-10	9-10
33	9-10	9-10	9-10	9-10	9-10	9-10	9-10	9-10
34	9-10	9-10	9-10	9-10	9-10	9-10	9-10	9-10
35	11-12	11-12	9-10	9-10	9-10	9-10	9-10	9-10
36	11-12	11-12	11-12	11-12	11-12	11-12	11-12	11-12
37	11-12	11-12	11-12	11-12	11-12	11-12	11-12	11-12
38	11-12	11-12	11-12	11-12	11-12	11-12	11-12	11-12
39	11-12	11-12	11-12	11-12	11-12	11-12	11-12	11-12
40	11-12	11-12	11-12	11-12	11-12	11-12	11-12	11-12
41	13-15	11-12	11-12	11-12	11-12	11-12	11-12	11-12
42	13-15	13-15	13-15	13-15	13-15	13-15	11-12	11-12
43	13-15	13-15	13-15	13-15	13-15	13-15	13-15	13-15
44	13-15	13-15	13-15	13-15	13-15	13-15	13-15	13-15
45	13-15	13-15	13-15	13-15	13-15	13-15	13-15	13-15
46	13-15	13-15	13-15	13-15	13-15	13-15	13-15	13-15
47	13-15	13-15	13-15	13-15	13-15	13-15	13-15	13-15
48	16	16	16	16	13-15	13-15	13-15	13-15
49	16	16	16	16	16	16	16	16
50	16	16	16	16	16	16	16	16

Number of unfamiliar words in sample

TABLE 2-2 CONTINUED

Number of sentences in sample

	25	26	27	28	29	30	31	32
0	1	1	1	1	1	1	1	1
1	1	1	1	1	1	1	1	1
2	1	1	1	1	1	1	1	1
3	1	1	1	1	1	1	1	1
4	1	1	1	1	1	1	1	1
5	1	1	1	1	1	1	1	1
6	2	2	2	2	2	2	1	1
7	2	2	2	2	2	2	2	2
8	2	2	2	2	2	2	2	2
9	3	3	3	3	2	2	2	2
10	3	3	3	3	3	3	3	3
11	3	3	3	3	3	3	3	3
12	3	3	3	3	3	3	3	3
13	4	4	3	3	3	3	3	3
14	4	4	4	4	4	4	4	4
15	4	4	4	4	4	4	4	4
16	4	4	4	4	4	4	4	4
17	4	4	4	4	4	4	4	4
18	4	4	4	4	4	4	4	4
19	5-6	5-6	5-6	5-6	5-6	5-6	5-6	5-6
20	5-6	5-6	5-6	5-6	5-6	5-6	5-6	5-6
21	5-6	5-6	5-6	5-6	5-6	5-6	5-6	5-6
22	5-6	5-6	5-6	5-6	5-6	5-6	5-6	5-6
23	5-6	5-6	5-6	5-6	5-6	5-6	5-6	5-6
24	7-8	7-8	7-8	7-8	7-8	7-8	7-8	5-6
25	7-8	7-8	7-8	7-8	7-8	7-8	7-8	7-8
26	7-8	7-8	7-8	7-8	7-8	7-8	7-8	7-8
27	7-8	7-8	7-8	7-8	7-8	7-8	7-8	7-8
28	7-8	7-8	7-8	7-8	7-8	7-8	7-8	7-8
29	7-8	7-8	7-8	7-8	7-8	7-8	7-8	7-8
30	9-10	9-10	9-10	7-8	7-8	7-8	7-8	7-8
31	9-10	9-10	9-10	9-10	9-10	9-10	9-10	9-10
32	9-10	9-10	9-10	9-10	9-10	9-10	9-10	9-10
33	9-10	9-10	9-10	9-10	9-10	9-10	9-10	9-10
34	9-10	9-10	9-10	9-10	9-10	9-10	9-10	9-10
35	9-10	9-10	9-10	9-10	9-10	9-10	9-10	9-10
36	9-10	9-10	9-10	9-10	9-10	9-10	9-10	9-10
37	11-12	11-12	11-12	11-12	11-12	11-12	11-12	11-12
38	11-12	11-12	11-12	11-12	11-12	11-12	11-12	11-12
39	11-12	11-12	11-12	11-12	11-12	11-12	11-12	11-12
40	11-12	11-12	11-12	11-12	11-12	11-12	11-12	11-12
41	11-12	11-12	11-12	11-12	11-12	11-12	11-12	11-12
42	11-12	11-12	11-12	11-12	11-12	11-12	11-12	11-12
43	13-15	13-15	13-15	13-15	13-15	13-15	13-15	13-15
44	13-15	13-15	13-15	13-15	13-15	13-15	13-15	13-15
45	13-15	13-15	13-15	13-15	13-15	13-15	13-15	13-15
46	13-15	13-15	13-15	13-15	13-15	13-15	13-15	13-15
47	13-15	13-15	13-15	13-15	13-15	13-15	13-15	13-15
48	13-15	13-15	13-15	13-15	13-15	13-15	13-15	13-15
49	16	16	16	16	13-15	13-15	13-15	13-15
50	16	16	16	16	16	16	16	16

Number of unfamiliar words in sample

TABLE 2-2 CONTINUED

Number of sentences in sample

	33	34	35	36	37	38
0	1	1	1	1	1	1
1	1	1	1	1	1	1
2	1	1	1	1	1	1
3	1	1	1	1	1	1
4	1	1	1	1	1	1
5	1	1	1	1	1	1
6	1	1	1	1	1	1
7	2	2	2	2	2	2
8	2	2	2	2	2	2
9	2	2	2	2	2	2
10	3	3	3	3	3	3
11	3	3	3	3	3	3
12	3	3	3	3	3	3
13	3	3	3	3	3	3
14	4	4	4	4	4	4
15	4	4	4	4	4	4
16	4	4	4	4	4	4
17	4	4	4	4	4	4
18	4	4	4	4	4	4
19	5-6	5-6	5-6	4	4	4
20	5-6	5-6	5-6	5-6	5-6	5-6
21	5-6	5-6	5-6	5-6	5-6	5-6
22	5-6	5-6	5-6	5-6	5-6	5-6
23	5-6	5-6	5-6	5-6	5-6	5-6
24	5-6	5-6	5-6	5-6	5-6	5-6
25	7-8	7-8	7-8	7-8	7-8	7-8
26	7-8	7-8	7-8	7-8	7-8	7-8
27	7-8	7-8	7-8	7-8	7-8	7-8
28	7-8	7-8	7-8	7-8	7-8	7-8
29	7-8	7-8	7-8	7-8	7-8	7-8
30	7-8	7-8	7-8	7-8	7-8	7-8
31	9-10	9-10	9-10	9-10	9-10	9-10
32	9-10	9-10	9-10	9-10	9-10	9-10
33	9-10	9-10	9-10	9-10	9-10	9-10
34	9-10	9-10	9-10	9-10	9-10	9-10
35	9-10	9-10	9-10	9-10	9-10	9-10
36	9-10	9-10	9-10	9-10	9-10	9-10
37	11-12	11-12	11-12	11-12	11-12	9-10
38	11-12	11-12	11-12	11-12	11-12	11-12
39	11-12	11-12	11-12	11-12	11-12	11-12
40	11-12	11-12	11-12	11-12	11-12	11-12
41	11-12	11-12	11-12	11-12	11-12	11-12
42	11-12	11-12	11-12	11-12	11-12	11-12
43	11-12	11-12	11-12	11-12	11-12	11-12
44	13-15	13-15	13-15	13-15	13-15	13-15
45	13-15	13-15	13-15	13-15	13-15	13-15
46	13-15	13-15	13-15	13-15	13-15	13-15
47	13-15	13-15	13-15	13-15	13-15	13-15
48	13-15	13-15	13-15	13-15	13-15	13-15
49	13-15	13-15	13-15	13-15	13-15	13-15
50	16	16	16	16	16	16

Number of unfamiliar words in sample

TABLE 2-2 CONTINUED

Number of sentences in sample

	39	40	41	42	43	44
0	1	1	1	1	1	1
1	1	1	1	1	1	1
2	1	1	1	1	1	1
3	1	1	1	1	1	1
4	1	1	1	1	1	1
5	1	1	1	1	1	1
6	1	1	1	1	1	1
7	2	2	2	2	2	2
8	2	2	2	2	2	2
9	2	2	2	2	2	2
10	3	3	3	3	3	3
11	3	3	3	3	3	3
12	3	3	3	3	3	3
13	3	3	3	3	3	3
14	4	4	3	3	3	3
15	4	4	4	4	4	4
16	4	4	4	4	4	4
17	4	4	4	4	4	4
18	4	4	4	4	4	4
19	4	4	4	4	4	4
20	5-6	5-6	5-6	5-6	5-6	5-6
21	5-6	5-6	5-6	5-6	5-6	5-6
22	5-6	5-6	5-6	5-6	5-6	5-6
23	5-6	5-6	5-6	5-6	5-6	5-6
24	5-6	5-6	5-6	5-6	5-6	5-6
25	7-8	7-8	7-8	7-8	7-8	7-8
26	7-8	7-8	7-8	7-8	7-8	7-8
27	7-8	7-8	7-8	7-8	7-8	7-8
28	7-8	7-8	7-8	7-8	7-8	7-8
29	7-8	7-8	7-8	7-8	7-8	7-8
30	7-8	7-8	7-8	7-8	7-8	7-8
31	9-10	9-10	9-10	9-10	9-10	9-10
32	9-10	9-10	9-10	9-10	9-10	9-10
33	9-10	9-10	9-10	9-10	9-10	9-10
34	9-10	9-10	9-10	9-10	9-10	9-10
35	9-10	9-10	9-10	9-10	9-10	9-10
36	9-10	9-10	9-10	9-10	9-10	9-10
37	9-10	9-10	9-10	9-10	9-10	9-10
38	11-12	11-12	11-12	11-12	11-12	11-12
39	11-12	11-12	11-12	11-12	11-12	11-12
40	11-12	11-12	11-12	11-12	11-12	11-12
41	11-12	11-12	11-12	11-12	11-12	11-12
42	11-12	11-12	11-12	11-12	11-12	11-12
43	11-12	11-12	11-12	11-12	11-12	11-12
44	13-15	13-15	13-15	13-15	13-15	13-15
45	13-15	13-15	13-15	13-15	13-15	13-15
46	13-15	13-15	13-15	13-15	13-15	13-15
47	13-15	13-15	13-15	13-15	13-15	13-15
48	13-15	13-15	13-15	13-15	13-15	13-15
49	13-15	13-15	13-15	13-15	13-15	13-15
50	16	16	16	16	16	16

Number of unfamiliar words in sample

TABLE 2-2 CONTINUED

Number of sentences in sample

	45	46	47	48	49	50
0	1	1	1	1	1	1
1	1	1	1	1	1	1
2	1	1	1	1	1	1
3	1	1	1	1	1	1
4	1	1	1	1	1	1
5	1	1	1	1	1	1
6	1	1	1	1	1	1
7	2	2	2	2	2	2
8	2	2	2	2	2	2
9	2	2	2	2	2	2
10	3	3	2	2	2	2
11	3	3	3	3	3	3
12	3	3	3	3	3	3
13	3	3	3	3	3	3
14	3	3	3	3	3	3
15	4	4	4	4	4	4
16	4	4	4	4	4	4
17	4	4	4	4	4	4
18	4	4	4	4	4	4
19	4	4	4	4	4	4
20	5-6	5-6	5-6	5-6	5-6	5-6
21	5-6	5-6	5-6	5-6	5-6	5-6
22	5-6	5-6	5-6	5-6	5-6	5-6
23	5-6	5-6	5-6	5-6	5-6	5-6
24	5-6	5-6	5-6	5-6	5-6	5-6
25	7-8	7-8	7-8	7-8	7-8	7-8
26	7-8	7-8	7-8	7-8	7-8	7-8
27	7-8	7-8	7-8	7-8	7-8	7-8
28	7-8	7-8	7-8	7-8	7-8	7-8
29	7-8	7-8	7-8	7-8	7-8	7-8
30	7-8	7-8	7-8	7-8	7-8	7-8
31	7-8	7-8	7-8	7-8	7-8	7-8
32	9-10	9-10	9-10	9-10	9-10	9-10
33	9-10	9-10	9-10	9-10	9-10	9-10
34	9-10	9-10	9-10	9-10	9-10	9-10
35	9-10	9-10	9-10	9-10	9-10	9-10
36	9-10	9-10	9-10	9-10	9-10	9-10
37	9-10	9-10	9-10	9-10	9-10	9-10
38	11-12	11-12	11-12	11-12	11-12	11-12
39	11-12	11-12	11-12	11-12	11-12	11-12
40	11-12	11-12	11-12	11-12	11-12	11-12
41	11-12	11-12	11-12	11-12	11-12	11-12
42	11-12	11-12	11-12	11-12	11-12	11-12
43	11-12	11-12	11-12	11-12	11-12	11-12
44	13-15	13-15	13-15	13-15	13-15	13-15
45	13-15	13-15	13-15	13-15	13-15	13-15
46	13-15	13-15	13-15	13-15	13-15	13-15
47	13-15	13-15	13-15	13-15	13-15	13-15
48	13-15	13-15	13-15	13-15	13-15	13-15
49	13-15	13-15	13-15	13-15	13-15	13-15
50	16	16	13-15	13-15	13-15	13-15

Number of unfamiliar words in sample

CHAPTER 3

Uses and Misuses of Readability Measurement

This chapter deals with proper and improper uses of the readability formulas, with particular reference to the new Dale-Chall formula. We consider such questions as the following:

- For what kinds of texts is the new formula suitable?
- What factors beside word and sentence difficulty should be assessed?
- How can texts best be matched to readers' characteristics? To their reading ability? To their purposes for reading?
- How hard or easy should texts be? For optimal comprehension when reading independently? When reading with teacher instruction or peer assistance? And for reading and language development?
- What is optimal difficulty for listening as compared to reading?

These questions are discussed to help the user of the new Dale-Chall formula gain a perspective on its use. Particularly because it is quite easy to apply, the user should be aware of the formula's limitations as well as its strengths. It is most important to keep in mind that it is a predictive instrument and that although the prediction is very high (.92), only 80 percent of the difficulty factors are accounted for. Thus, the user should not expect a one-to-one relationship between predictions and reality. (See Chapters 4 and 5 for detailed evidence of statistical validity.) The formula can be applied easily (by hand or by computer), but knowing when it can and cannot be used, and what the scores mean, requires knowledge, experience, and judgment. This chapter is designed to give users some of these basic understandings.

Matching Texts to Readers and Their Purposes

The purpose of readability assessment is to effect a "best match" between intended readers and texts. A readability formula is a tool for predicting the difficulty of text. It tells how hard the material probably is in terms of relative difficulty or in relation to the reading ability of prospective readers. But it does not tell how hard it *should* be. For that, one needs to know the reading abilities of the prospective readers, their background knowledge with regard to the content of the text, and the purpose of the material's use (whether it will serve as a textbook that will be enhanced by a teacher's instruction or whether it is to be read independently). The more one knows about the prospective readers' abilities and purposes, the better the match can be. Thus, to make a best match between readers and text it is necessary to obtain information about the intended readers, information about the readability of the material, and information about the purpose for its use.

Information on the intended readers might include — when available — their reading ability, their previous knowledge and interest in the topic, and how the material is to be read — whether independently or as part of instruction by a teacher.

A student's reading ability may be estimated by scores or bands on a recently administered reading test.[1] If these are not available, estimates of reading ability may be made by noting the readability of the books, magazines, and newspaper they read. For adults, the last school grade reached may be used to estimate reading ability, although the estimates may be higher than found when tests are used.[2]

When the topics of texts are familiar to the intended readers, and when readers find them of interest, they usually find them easier to read. Unfamiliar texts and those less interesting will generally be harder to read. Also, the same texts read with assistance from a teacher are easier to read than those read without help. Material that is to be read independently should be on a lower level than material to be read with the help of a teacher or a more knowledgeable peer.

Thus, optimal difficulty comes from an interaction between the text, the reader, and his/her purpose in reading. The following discussion addresses more specifically the easy/hard issue. How hard or easy should texts be? What is an optimal match for comprehension? For learning?

Generally, most readability researchers have considered an optimal match to be text on the same readability level as the reading level of the readers for independent reading.

Recent research indicates, however, that when used for instructional purposes, the text may be somewhat above the student's level to encourage optimal development of reading comprehension. (See Chall, Conard, & Harris, 1977; Chall, Jacobs, & Baldwin, 1990; Chall & Conard, 1991; Hayes, Wolfer, & Wolfe, 1993. See also Vygotsky, 1978, who proposed that optimal difficulty for learning be at a level of "proximal development" for learners — i.e., above their level of development, and not below, when assisted by a teacher or more knowledgeable peers.) For elemen-

---

[1] There has been much discussion about the meaning and validity of the "exact" grade level scores (e.g., 3.8, 7.4) on standardized reading tests. Nearly all test publishers now report individual scores as a band, or range, as is done in both the original and new Dale-Chall readability formulas. It is therefore suggested that the band or range be used.

[2] Before "automatic" or "age level promotions" became standard practice (about 40-50 years ago), the last school grade reached was a reasonable estimate of reading ability. It still is quite useful. Because many unskilled readers are promoted, the reading levels of adolescents and adults may be lower than their last grade reached.

tary and high school students, reading achievement improves when the books used for instruction (with teacher and/or peer assistance) are challenging — i.e., somewhat above their reading levels, not lower.

It would appear, then, that instructional materials, particularly those from which students receive instruction, need to be sufficiently challenging to produce optimal long-term growth in reading. This is particularly true when teachers can give assistance in the background knowledge, the new vocabulary, and in the kind of thinking required.

The new Dale-Chall readability scores, as well as those from most traditional formulas, can be viewed as predicting the level suitable for independent reading, since the passages were tested during independent silent reading, without teachers' instruction or assistance. However, if the text is to be used for instruction (i.e., students receive help from a teacher), the optimal text readability could be harder than the students' tested reading level.

Materials to be read by the general public — e.g., medicine inserts, instructions for filing income tax forms, instructions for using household machines — should, on the other hand, be as easy as possible to convey accurate information to most of the adult population, even those with limited reading ability.

Books used for instruction in elementary and high school should inform but also enhance the students' language and reading ability. Textbooks generally serve the purpose of developing the students' knowledge in a particular field as well as enhancing their language and reading ability. Therefore, it would seem that textbooks, when used with instruction and guidance from teachers and/or more advanced peers, may be on a level that is somewhat above students' tested reading levels. (See Chall, Conard, & Harris, 1977; Chall & Conard, 1991; Chall, Jacobs, & Baldwin, 1990; Hayes, Wolfer, & Wolfe, 1993.)[3]

Optimal Difficulty for Listening as Compared to Reading

Generally, the Dale-Chall formula can be used to estimate listening comprehension difficulty as it does reading comprehension difficulty. For placing selections in an order of increasing difficulty, the ranks will tend to be the same. However, for estimating the most appropriate match for listening and for reading, one finds differences.

For listening comprehension, texts at reading levels below about an 8th grade will usually be easier to understand when heard than when read. This is because

---

[3] There has been a preference for "easier" texts from the early 1920s and many researchers and teachers still prefer easier texts. However, our research (noted above) and that of Hayes and his associates indicate that when more challenging materials are used for instruction, over many years, students achieve higher scores in reading and language development than those using less challenging materials.

This is particularly true for books at a 4th grade level and higher which contain ever more difficult, abstract and technicalwords, and more difficult concepts. Thus reading with an instructor, at a level beyond that of the student's present development (his/her reading level or Vygotsky's level of proximal development), the student has a better chance of learning more difficult concepts and more difficult words — the strongest factor in reading achievement and reading comprehension difficulty. Using books that are on the student's present level or below, helps in the development of fluency and rate, but not as much in reading comprehension.

spoken language develops faster than written language until about 8th grade. From about an 8th to a 12th grade level, the same texts will be of about equal difficulty when heard as when read. Beyond a 12th grade level, the same text may be harder to understand when heard than when read (Chall, 1983b; Sticht, Beck, Hauke, Kleiman & James, 1974).

For What Kinds of Texts is the New Formula Suitable?

The new Dale-Chall formula is appropriate for use with connected texts including articles and books — fiction and non-fiction. Most textbooks in science, social studies, literature and the humanities can be appropriately assessed. Also appropriate for analyses are articles in newspapers and magazines, and technical reports.

In general, technical materials in mathematics that contain many numbers, symbols, and equations are not well served by the formula. Poetry is often poorly assessed by the new Dale-Chall formula and by most traditional measures. Because of metaphorical language in poetry which uses familiar words, the readability scores obtained are often underestimates of their true difficulty. In this connection, see Taylor (1953) on cloze.

The new formula can be used to rate passages at reading levels 1 to college graduate level. The original formula, however, rated passages only at reading levels 4 and above. The lower ratings were made possible by the Bormuth criterion passages, which included selections below the 4th reading level. With extrapolation, we were able to have the new formula discriminate between reading levels 1, 2 and 3. Although the new formula can be used to estimate difficulty at these levels, the degree of confidence is not as high as it is for discriminating between reading levels 4 through 16+.

What Factors Besides Word and Sentence Difficulty Should Be Assessed?

The new Dale-Chall readability estimates are enhanced by judgments about other factors which are known to be associated with readability, but are not directly measured by the formula. These are noted below, in the instructions, and on the worksheets. (See Chapter 2.) We suggest these qualitative judgments be taken into account when making an appropriate match between readers and text. Indeed, if the text is favorable on these qualities, it may actually be less difficult than the readability score estimates. If the text is low on these qualities, it may be more difficult to read than the formula estimates.

- Unfamiliar and technical words are used well in context and/or are clearly defined in the text, in footnotes, or in glossaries.
- Unfamiliar concepts are explained in terms of the reader's previous knowledge.
- Chapters, sections, and the entire book are well organized, with use of headings, questions, and other aids to improve structure.

- Questions are inserted in the text preceding, within, or following teaching units.
- Illustrations to explain difficult ideas are placed close to the text they amplify and contain helpful captions.

These are to be "checked off" as characteristics of the text, with an indication of the degree to which they are found in the text.

It should be noted that these qualitative characteristics enhance comprehension and retention in textbooks and instructional materials, particularly at levels 4 and above. Further, these may not be reflected in the two factors in the new Dale-Chall formula. Hence, their consideration adds another dimension to the readability scores. They are not substitutes for the readability scores. They are a supplement to them.

Judgments of Cognitive and Structural Features

Readability estimates are enhanced by taking into account cognitive and structural factors known to be associated with readability, but which are not directly measured by readability formulas. If the text has good organization and explains ideas well, it may be less difficult than the readability formula estimates. If the text is weak on these qualities, it may be more difficult to read than the formula suggests. Estimates of organization and idea difficulty are not substitutes for readability scores. They are supplements to them. (See Worksheet C.)

The Use of Formulas for Writing and Editing

Readability formulas have also been used by writers, editors, and publishers to write, rewrite, and revise reading materials to specified readability levels. This has been criticized because the lowering of readability scores has not always produced better comprehension of the supposedly easier texts, and it has also been reported to lead to more ambiguous writing. Mechanically shortening sentences has been reported to result in loss of cause and effect relationship (Davison and Kantor, 1980). Indeed, the early students of readability also cautioned against the use of readability formulas as rules for writing or rewriting (Horn, 1930). Readability formulas are valid, they claimed, for predicting reading difficulty, but they are too limited when used as rules for writing.

However, readability *principles* rather than readability formulas can be helpful in revising and writing materials for readers of specified reading levels. An analogy with reading tests may be useful here, since readability formulas are in many ways similar to standardized reading tests. A readability formula assesses the difficulty of reading material much as a standardized reading test measures the reading ability of students. Similar to standardized reading tests, readability formulas deal only with samples of the text and important aspects of difficulty, not with all aspects of it. Scores from readability formulas, as scores from standardized reading tests, are based on only the most potent predictors of reading difficulty. Since both readability measures and reading tests measure only limited aspects of readability and reading ability, judgment is needed for full interpretation. Also, to effect a change in true readability or reading ability, more than the few factors measured need to be modified.

It has therefore been common among readability researchers to call for caution in the use of readability formulas as guides for writing and editing. From the early years of readability research, rewriting to desired readability standards was viewed in terms of using guidelines and helpful techniques, rather than changing words and sentences to obtain lower scores (Dale & Hager, 1950; Flesch, 1949; Gunning, 1952, 1968). A readability formula is suggested for assessing a manuscript and for sensitizing writers to the factors of difficulty. Writing and rewriting for greater readability are presented in qualitative terms of organization, conceptual difficulty, defining of technical and difficult words, and the like. (See Chapter 10.)

Many developers of readability formulas have written guides on readable writing (see Chapter 10). Yet in spite of these cautions and broader guides, there has been concern with the mechanical use of readability measures for editing and writing. Some writers seek to simplify reading difficulty by "chopping" long sentences and substituting more familiar for less familiar words. In fact, a review of the early studies on the effects of such changes found that small changes in words and sentences added little to improving comprehension. Very large changes in word difficulty and sentence complexity did increase reading comprehension. The most effective revisions in terms of improved comprehension, however, were those that changed the organizational structure, the appeal, and other qualitative aspects in addition to the vocabulary and sentence structure. (See Klare, 1984, for a sensitive analysis of the readability formulas for writing, and also an earlier review of the research by Chall, 1958.)

The Varied Uses of Readability Measurement

One of the earliest uses of readability was in the selection of children's trade or library books to match their reading abilities.

Some 350 library books with their readability scores were included in the volume *The Right Book for the Right Child* (Washburne, 1942), a list of books to assist librarians, teachers, and parents in matching books to children's reading abilities. More recently George Spache has published *Good Reading for Poor Readers* (1962, revised 1979), containing the readability scores of several hundred books.

Classic readability measurement has been used widely since its earliest development in the 1920s. It has been used to select reading and subject matter textbooks to match the reading abilities of groups and individuals, in the development of beginner books and high-interest, low-reading-level books. It has also been used in the development of adapted classics.

Widely read children's newspapers and magazines such as *My Weekly Reader* and children's magazines published by *The National Geographic* have used readability measurement, together with field testing, to develop publications readable by children of different ages and grades. Readability formulas have also been used in the development of children's encyclopedias such as *World Book* and *The New Book of*

Knowledge. They have been used to effect a better match between general adult newspapers and magazines and their readers, and between corporation reports and other specialized materials and their readers.

Readability measurement has been used to estimate the reading level required to pass given portions of the Scholastic Aptitude Test and state minimum competency tests (Chall, Conard, & Harris, 1977; Chall, Freeman, & Levy, 1982). Classic readability measurement has also been used in legal suits as evidence regarding the comprehension difficulty of legal documents and whether they could be understood by the special groups for which they were intended. Classic readability measurements with qualitative analyses of conceptual difficulties and organization have been used to assess and modify patent medicine inserts to match the reading abilities of those most likely to use the information (Harris-Sharples, 1982).

The armed forces have used readability measurement to estimate the reading ability needed for given jobs through an analysis of the difficulty levels of the publications used in the different jobs (Sticht, Caylor, Fox, Hauke, James, Snyder, & Kern, 1973).

There has also been considerable use of readability measurement and principles in the simplification of the W-2 federal tax forms by the Document Design Center of the American Institute on Research.

Industry has been making increased use of readability measures to assess the readability of its annual reports, proxy cards, and other means of communicating with the public. It has been using readability to improve communication with employees, particularly those with lower reading abilities and skills. It is working both to improve the reading skills of employees and to simplify the manuals and written instructions targeted for them (Venezky, 1982).

Readability measurement has been used by museums and aquariums to improve the readability of their labels and signs. A museum specializing in dinosaurs in Washington uses labels on a fifth to sixth grade reading level to permit children, young people, and adults to read and understand the labels and instructions easily.

Section II

THE SCIENTIFIC BASIS OF THE NEW DALE-CHALL FORMULA

Section II (Chapters 4 and 5) is concerned with the validation of the new Dale-Chall Readability Formula. It presents data on the standardization of the formula as well as comparisons of the new readability scores with other, independent measures of difficulty.

Chapter 4 presents correlations of the Dale-Chall word and sentence factors with the difficulties of criterion passages from four classic readability formulas. Development of the new formula was based on these correlations. Using new word familiarity and sentence length counts, the new formula correlates .92 with cloze comprehension scores.

Chapter 5 presents the correlations of the new Dale-Chall scores with independent measures of difficulty — scores from standardized reading tests, the reading proficiency levels of the National Assessments of Educational Progress, expert judgments of difficulty, and the Fry readability scores.

Overall, the validation data indicate that the new Dale-Chall formula predicts difficulty at a very high level of accuracy, with a multiple correlation of .92, accounting for over 80 percent of the variation in text difficulty.

The high predictive validity of the new formula is confirmed by the high associations between formula scores and the difficulty of selections on recently published reading tests.

CHAPTER 4

Standardization of the New Dale-Chall Formula

In this chapter, we present the procedures used to develop the new Dale-Chall Readability Formula, along with evidence of its validity.

We had several objectives for the new formula:

1. To select a stronger set of criterion passages.[1] Studies by Bormuth (1967, 1968), Porter and Popp (1975), and others suggested that a set of criterion passages whose difficulty was assessed by a cloze test[2] would be more productive than a set of criterion passages whose difficulty was established by a multiple choice comprehension test — the method used in the original Dale-Chall formula.

2. To use an updated word list. Test results from Dale and O'Rourke (1976, 1981) suggested some changes in the vocabulary knowledge of contemporary students as compared to those of forty years ago when the original formula was developed.

3. To modify some of the rules for the unfamiliar word count and the count of words and sentences. Since the original formula was published, studies have suggested that computations could be simplified while maintaining high predictions (Goltz, 1964).

4. To simplify all aspects of the original formula in order to gain greater efficiency.

---

[1] Criterion passages are needed to develop readability measures — whether classic or new. They are sets of passages of increasing levels of difficulty as determined by independent tests of comprehension, cloze, rate, or expert judgment. The text features that can best predict the independent measure of difficulty are combined to develop a readability measure.

[2] A cloze test uses the correct completion of the deleted words in a passage as evidence of understanding the selection. Thus, the more deletions correctly filled in for a selection, the better the comprehension. Also, the higher the percentage of correct fill-ins by a panel of readers, the more readable the text is considered.

Selecting the New Criterion Passages

The original Dale-Chall formula (1948), like the Flesch (1948) and Lorge (1939) before it, was validated on the McCall-Crabbs *Standard Test Lessons in Reading* (1926). At the time these formulas were developed, the McCall-Crabbs passages represented the most extensive collection of graded reading passages available at elementary and high school levels based on multiple-choice comprehension questions. Later editions of the McCall-Crabbs *Standard Test Lessons*, e.g., the 1950 and 1961 editions, did not seem to improve their strength as criterion passages (MacGinitie & Tretiak, 1971; Miller & Coleman, 1967). More promising results were reported, however, in studies that used criterion passages based on cloze tests — supplying deleted words (Bormuth, 1969). In view of these findings, we decided to search for an alternative criterion to the McCall-Crabbs.

We sought a criterion that represented a variety of content and a wide range of difficulty, based on a sound, acceptable test of comprehension. To find a criterion that best met those requirements, we elicited the cooperation of prominent researchers in the field of readability.[3] Their suggestions and their offers to make their data available to us led to our decision to experiment with four different sets of criterion passages — those of Bormuth (1971), Miller and Coleman (1967), MacGinitie and Tretiak (1971), and Caylor, Sticht, Fox and Ford (1973).

Table 4-1 presents basic data on the four criteria — the subjects who read the passages, the sources of the passages, the numbers of selections, and how difficulty was determined. The four sets of criterion passages each contained from 12 to 80 passages which were read by readers ranging from a third to a college graduate reading level. Reading comprehension was determined by cloze, multiple-choice comprehension tests, judgments of difficulty, etc. The passages varied from elementary school instructional materials to college textbooks and military regulations and manuals.

Selecting Formula Factors

Many different text characteristics, perhaps 100 or more, have been studied as possible indicators of reading difficulty in classic readability studies (Chall, 1958, 1981). Most of these factors represent two broad aspects of comprehension difficulty — vocabulary or semantic factors, and sentence complexity or syntactic factors. The original Dale-Chall formula is based on these two factors. *Semantic* factors refer, in this context, to unfamiliar words, that is, words not on the Dale List of 3,000 words known to 80 percent of 4th graders tested. *Syntactic* factors refer to the average length of sentences. In the development of the original formula, it was found that adding such factors as prepositional phrases and personal references contributed little to the overall predictive capability derived from words and sentences (Dale & Chall, 1948).

---

[3] We are deeply indebted to John Bormuth, Edmund Coleman, Albert Harris, George Klare, Walter MacGinitie, and Thomas Sticht for their prompt responses to our inquiries. Their help was invaluable in this project as well as their generosity in making their data available to us.

Table 4-1: Four Sets of Criterion Passages Considered
in the Standardization of the New Dale-Chall Formula

	Bormuth	**Miller and Coleman**	**MacGinitie and Tretiak**	**Caylor et al.**
Date of Study	1971	1967	1971	1973
Subjects	285 elementary and high school students: 3rd to 12th grades	479 college students	College and graduate students	395 Air Force trainees
Sources of Passages	School instructional materials including subject areas: biology, chemistry, civics, current news, economics, geography, history, literature, mathematics, physics	Selections from *McCall-Crabbs Standard Test Lessons in Reading (1961)* and textbooks in psychology and literature.	Selections from *McCall-Crabbs Standard Test Lessons in Reading (1961)*	Selections from *Regulations and Job Manual for Military Occupation Specialist*
Number of Passages	32	36	80	12
How difficulty level was determined	Cloze scores	Cloze scores and subjective ranking	Grade-level scores on the McCall-Crabbs	Cloze scores and scores from other readability formulas

We reviewed the more recent work on readability that stresses the importance of such cognitive and organizational factors as idea difficulty and diversity, text cohesion, and organization. Some of these are suggested for qualitative assessment in the new Dale-Chall formula. (See Chapters 6, 7, and 8, as well as Chapter 2.)

John Bormuth's extensive work in readability measurement was examined closely. In a 1964 study, Bormuth tested and correlated some 47 readability variables with his criterion passages to see if adding any to existing formulas would improve their predictive power. The 47 variables that Bormuth used included traditional measures of readability (i.e., sentence length, word length, words not on the Dale list of 3,000 words) and also many new measures of syntactic complexity. From among these new factors, promising results were found for letter redundancy, and form-class ratios (ratios among the eight parts of speech).

These new linguistic factors, however, added little to Bormuth's overall predictions of difficulty (1964), and they were not included in subsequent formulas. The Bormuth Cloze Mean Formula published in 1971 (used in the construction of the

Degrees of Reading Power [DRP] Test)[4] is based on counts of three factors: 1) words not on the original Dale List of 3,000 (Dale & Chall, 1948), 2) average sentence length, and 3) average word length in letters. Thus, the Bormuth Cloze Mean Formula uses the two factors from the original Dale-Chall formula, and an additional word length factor. Bormuth's research seems to suggest, also, that the new, more theoretically innovative syntactic measures contributed no more to the overall prediction of readability than the traditional and easier-to-measure average sentence length.

Similar findings were reported by MacGinitie and Tretiak (1971). To revise the Lorge formula (1949), MacGinitie and Tretiak evaluated the predictive strength of various syntactic measures — classic and new — with the comprehension scores from the 1960s edition of the McCall-Crabbs Standard Test Lessons. They found that the newer syntactic measures were so highly correlated with the classic average sentence length that they added little to the prediction of syntactic difficulty. Indeed, they found average sentence length to be the best predictor of syntactic difficulty.

These studies led to our decision to retain the traditional syntactic factor for the new formula — average sentence length.

Modifications of the Dale List

The vocabulary factor in the original formula was based on the Dale List of 3,000 Words known to 80 percent of 4th graders in the early 1940s. Since more than forty years had passed, an update of the list was needed to more accurately reflect the vocabulary knowledge of contemporary readers.

For the past several decades, Edgar Dale and his associate, Joseph O'Rourke, have tested the vocabulary knowledge of students from Grade 4 through college level on thousands of words. The results of this extensive testing have been published in *The Living Word Vocabulary* (Dale & O'Rourke, 1976 and 1981). The updated list of 3,000 words used for the new formula was based on the larger list and includes words known by 80 percent of 4th grade students in the 1980s. Some general changes in the words known by present-day 4th graders as compared to the 4th graders of the 1940s were found. Today's 4th graders know more words of a general, scientific, and abstract nature. The 4th graders of the 1940s knew more agricultural and domestic words. Additional information on the changes in the Dale list of 3,000 words is presented in Chapter 9.

Modifications in Rules

Overall, changes in rules and instructions were based on two objectives. First, the rules should be more clearly and explicitly stated to enhance accuracy and efficiency. Second, ambiguity should be reduced as much as possible so that uncer-

---

[4] See College Entrance Examination Board, 1980 and later editions, for DRP's modified cloze test of reading comprehension, for elementary and high school, which uses Bormuth's 1971 readability formula.

tainties would be minimized. Details of the changes are discussed below.

Fewer Samples

Various studies had been undertaken since the publication of the original Dale-Chall formula to determine the optimal number of samples needed to obtain scores consistent with that for an entire book or document. The original formula recommended taking samples from every tenth page.

Since the new formula is not fundamentally different from the old in the factors measured and in the relative potency of each, we used various findings on the sampling reliability of the original formula as evidence for the sampling reliability of the new.

The results of a variety of these sampling studies are summarized in Appendix A, page 144. Overall, they indicate that significantly fewer samples could be used. (See Chapter 2, page 7, for the optimal number of samples recommended.)

Simpler Computations

The number of computations required for the new formula has been reduced. Soon after the original formula was published, George Klare (1952) developed a computation table (the Klare Table) for the original formula from which readability raw scores could be obtained. The raw score was then easily converted into corrected grade levels using a table provided by the authors. The Klare Table was included by the Ohio State University Press in a reprint of the instructions for using the original (Dale & Chall, 1948). Later, Goltz (1964) published a table that allowed the two factors of the original Dale-Chall formula to be converted directly into corrected grade levels.

Another simplification is the use of exact 100-word samples for counting the number of unfamiliar words and the number of sentences. These are then directly converted into cloze scores[5] or reading levels. Thus, analysts do not need to calculate the percent of unfamiliar words and average sentence length as in the original formula.

Two other changes were made in the rules for counting sentences. In the original formula, there had been no mention of how to count topic headings that frequently appear in educational materials. Although these headings are seldom punctuated as sentences, it was decided to count them as sentences in the new formula since they serve as an aid to reading by offering a concise statement of the content to follow. Therefore, topic headings are counted as separate sentences. Since they are usually shorter than complete sentences, it seemed reasonable to expect a lower average sentence length in a sample that included a topic heading.

---

[5] Cloze scores indicate the percentage of correct words inserted for the deletions in a passage. The greater the correct insertions, the better the comprehension and the higher the cloze score. This cloze score was included for several reasons, such as the increasing questioning of grade level scores for use in standardized tests and in readability measurement. Cloze scores were more generally accepted. Another reason why cloze scores may be preferred by some is that they provide continuous scores that may be useful for showing gains and progress for teaching and for research. Since the reading level scores use broader bands or ranges, they may not be as useful for showing differences in readability of different texts and changes over time.

Changes in the Unfamiliar Word Count

The new Dale-Chall formula has added a count of familiar and unfamiliar numbers from the work of Ted Kilty (1979).

Overall, the count of unfamiliar words has been made easier by omitting references to grammatical classifications as was done in the original. In the interests of simplicity, the new formula notes only specified endings which, when added to a base word, indicate that it is to be counted as familiar or unfamiliar.

Standardization Procedures

The scoring system for each set of criterion passages used in the development of the new formula follows:

Bormuth (1971) (32 passages)

1. Cloze Mean Score — the mean score of students who completed cloze tests constructed from the passage, every fifth word deleted.
2. Grade Placement Score — the average grade placement of students who achieved 55% correct on cloze tests constructed from the passage.
3. Grade Placement Score — the average grade placement of students who achieved 45% correct on cloze tests constructed from the passage.
4. Grade Placement Score — the average grade placement of students who achieved 35% correct on cloze tests constructed from the passage.

Miller-Coleman (1967) (36 passages)

1. The average percent of correct responses on cloze tests, every fifth word deleted.
2. A rank order score derived by averaging the subjective ranks assigned to each passage by fourteen judges.

Caylor et al. (1973) (12 passages)

1. Reading Grade Level Score — the reading grade level from the USAG Intelligence Achievement Tests achieved by 50% of the subjects who score at least 35% correct on cloze tests constructed from the passage.
2. Cloze Mean Score — the average percent of correct responses on cloze tests.

MacGinitie and Tretiak (1971) (80 passages)

1. Grade Level Score — the grade level equivalent of 75% correct on multiple choice tests from the McCall-Crabbs Standardized Test Lessons in Reading, 1961.

The following factors were correlated with each of the four sets of *criterion passages* as noted above:

• Original Dale-Chall formula scores based on original rules for words and

sentence length.
- New Dale-Chall formula scores based on new word list and new word and sentence counts.

Statistical comparisons (correlations) were run between each set of the four criterion passages and the above readability factors. (See Tables 4-2, 4-4, 4-5 and 4-6 for the correlations.)

Table 4-2: Correlations of Original and New Dale-Chall Factors with Bormuth Scores[6]
(N= 32 passages)

Score		(1)	(2)	(3)	(4)	(5)	(6)	(7)	(8)[7]
(1)	Original formula unfamiliar word count	1.0000	.5863	.9463	.5621	.8147	.7951	.7946	-0.853
(2)	Original formula average sentence length			.6825	.9771	.7955	.7751	.7020	-.7865
(3)	New formula unfamiliar word count				.6694	.8622	.8352	.8070	-.8879
(4)	New formula average sentence length					.7751	.7421	.6526	-.7728
(5)	Bormuth 35% grade placement						.9852	.9338	-.9748
(6)	Bormuth 45% grade placement							.9757	-.9639
(7)	Bormuth 55% grade placement								-.9210
(8)	Bormuth cloze mean score								1.0000

Note: All correlations are significantly greater than 0 (P<.01)

[6] See Table 4-1 for explanation of Bormuth scores and scores for three other sets of criterion passages.
[7] The Bormuth cloze mean score correlates negatively with the various readability factors because higher cloze scores stand for easier texts, not for harder texts as with reading levels.

Results

From Table 4-2 we note the correlations of the original and new Dale-Chall formula factors with 4 types of comprehension scores from Bormuth. Note the high correlations of the word factors, whether based on the original or the new Dale list, with the Bormuth scores. The highest correlation is for the new unfamiliar word count, based on the new Dale List of 3,000 words, and the Bormuth mean cloze

Table 4-3: Correlations of Original and New Dale-Chall Factors
with Miller-Coleman Scores
(N = 36 passages)

Score		(1)	(2)	(3)	(4)	(5)	(6)
(1)	Original formula unfamiliar word count	1.0000	0.5166	0.9753	0.5054	-0.8858	0.8898
(2)	Original formula average sentence length			0.5433	0.9059	-0.5694	0.6013
(3)	New formula unfamiliar word count				0.5011	-0.8614	0.8731
(4)	New formula average sentence length					-0.5514	0.5978
(5)	Coleman cloze mean score						-0.9408
(6)	Coleman rank order						1.0000

Note: All correlations are significantly greater than 0 (P<.01)

Table 4-4: Correlations of Original and New Dale-Chall Factors with
MacGinitie-Tretiak Scores
(N = 80)

Score		(1)	(2)	(3)	(4)	(5)
(1)	Original formula unfamiliar word count	1.0000	0.2479	0.8180	0.1940	0.6847
(2)	Original formula average sentence length			0.3424	0.8312	0.3306
(3)	New formula unfamiliar word count				0.3020	0.6366
(4)	New formula average sentence length					0.2597
(5)	MacGinitie 75% grade level score on McCall-Crabbs (1961)					1.0000

Note: All correlations are significantly greater than 0 (P<.01) with one exception: (1) with (2), P<.025

score (.89). This is appreciably higher than the correlation of .68 of the unfamiliar word count of the original formula with the McCall-Crabbs Test Lessons (Dale & Chall, 1948). It would seem that a cloze criterion as well as the updated Dale List with the new instructions raised the correlations, as had been anticipated.

As with the original formula, the sentence factors are less predictive than the word factors. They have lower correlations with the Bormuth cloze scores. However, the new sentence length count correlates .77 with the Bormuth cloze mean score — considerably higher than the correlation of .47 between the original sentence count and the reading comprehension scores on the McCall-Crabbs test lessons (Dale & Chall, 1948). Of interest, too, are the high correlations among Bormuth's four measures of text difficulty.

Table 4-3 presents the correlations of old and new Dale-Chall readability factors with the Miller-Coleman difficulty scores. The correlations are similar to those for Caylor et al. (see Table 4-5), with higher correlations for the word factors (the original and new) and somewhat lower for the original and new sentence length factors.

Table 4-4 contains the correlations of old and new Dale-Chall factors with the MacGinitie-Tretiak reading comprehension scores on the 1961 McCall-Crabbs passages. It is interesting to note that the correlations of both the word and sentence factors with the McCall-Crabbs comprehension scores are lower than those for the other three sets of criterion passages which used cloze tests to measure comprehen-

Table 4-5: Correlations of Original and New Dale-Chall Factors with
Caylor et al. Scores
(N = 12)

Score		(1)	(2)	(3)	(4)	(5)	(6)
(1)	Original formula unfamiliar word count	1.0000	0.3713	0.9195(*)	0.3915	0.8860(*)	-0.8745(*)
(2)	Original formula average sentence length			0.4398	0.9435(*)	0.4962	-0.4551
(3)	New formula unfamiliar word count				0.5269(**)	0.8618(*)	-0.5441(**)
(4)	New formula average sentence length					0.5201(**)	-0.4918
(5)	Caylor cloze test score						-0.9943(*)
(6)	Caylor rank order						1.0000

Note: (*) P ‹ .005; (**) P ‹ .05; others n.s.

sion. The word factors based on the old and new Dale word lists are .68 and .64. For the original and new sentence factors the correlations are .33 and .26, at 75 percent comprehension. These correlations are considerably below those from the other three sets of criterion passages. They are closer to correlations found for the original Dale-Chall formula and others based on the 1922 McCall-Crabbs passages (Chall, 1958).

Table 4-5 presents the correlations of the old and new Dale-Chall factors with the Caylor et al. cloze mean scores and reading levels. As for the Bormuth, the original and new Dale-Chall word factors have the highest correlations with the Caylor measures of difficulty. The sentence length correlations with the Caylor difficulty scores are lower than the word familiarity correlations, as would be expected.

Table 4-6 presents the correlations of the original and new Dale-Chall formula factors with the four criteria (Bormuth, Miller-Coleman, MacGinitie-Tretiak, Caylor et al.). We note that the highest correlations were with the Bormuth scores, and especially with Bormuth's cloze mean scores. The factor with the highest correla-

Table 4-6: Correlations of Predictor Variables in Original and New Formula with Four Sets of Criterion Scores[8]

Criterion Scores	Original Formula		New Formula	
	Unfamiliar word count	Average sentence length	Unfamiliar word count	Average sentence length
Bormuth (N = 32)			**Note: All sig P<.01**	
Cloze mean	-.8537	-.7865	-.8879	-.7728
35% grade placement	.8147	.7955	.8622	.7751
45% grade placement	.7951	.7751	.8352	.7421
55% grade placement	.7946	.7020	.8070	.6526
Miller-Coleman (N = 36)			**Note: All sig P<.01**	
Cloze test scores	-.8858	-.5694	-.8615	-.5514
Subjective rank order	.8898	.6013	.8731	.5978
MacGinitie-Tretiak (N = 80)			**Note: All sig P<.01**	
75% grade placement	.6847	.3306	.6366	.2597
Caylor, Sticht, Fox, Ford (N = 12)				
Cloze mean	-.8745 P<.01	-.4551 n.s.	-.8441 P<.01	-.4918 n.s.
Reading grade level	.8860 P<.01	.4962 n.s.	.8618 P<.01	.5201 P<.05

[8] Scores given by each author are explained in Table 4-1.

tion was the new unfamiliar word count (.89), based on the new Dale List of 3,000 words and the new rules for counting unfamiliar words and numbers. The sentence length factor correlated somewhat lower with the four sets of criterion passages — .79 for the original sentence count and .77 for the new. The difference between the original and new sentence counts is slight and justifies the use of the less time-consuming exact 100-word samples.

The correlations with the Caylor et al. and Miller-Coleman criteria are quite high, but lower than the Bormuth. The correlations with the MacGinitie criterion scores are the lowest.

Table 4-6 also indicates that overall, higher correlations were found for criterion passages that used cloze tests as compared to those that used multiple choice tests. Although the exact correlations seem to vary with the type of test used, the relative strengths of the factors remain the same. The word factor correlates higher than the sentence length factor with all four sets of criterion passages.

Table 4-7 presents the multiple correlations[9] of the original and new Dale-Chall formulas with the four criterion measures. The multiple correlations for the new formula — new word and sentence counts — ranged from .71 to .92. The highest (.92) was for the Bormuth cloze mean scores.

Table 4-7 indicates that the Bormuth criterion passages yielded the highest

Table 4-7: Multiple Correlations of Combined Factors in Original and New Dale-Chall Formulas with the Four Criterion Measures

	N=32 Bormuth Scores				N=36 Miller-Coleman Scores		N=80 MacGinitie-Tretiak Scores	N=12 Caylor, Sticht, Fox, Ford Scores	
Vocabulary & Sentence Factors Combined	35% Correct	45% Correct	55% Correct	Cloze Mean Score	Cloze Scores	Subjective Rank	75% Correct	Cloze Mean Score	Reading Grade Level
Original Dale-Chall word and sentence count	.904	.882	.846	.924	.895	.905	.705	.886	.094
New Dale-Chall Formula: New Dale List, new unfamiliar word count, and new sentence count	0.902 All sig P<.01	.871	.821	.920	0.872 P<.01	.893	0.64 P<.01	0.846 P<.01	.865

---

[9] Correlations based on the combined word and sentence variables with the criterion passages.

multiple correlations with the new Dale-Chall word and sentence factors. Of the four Bormuth scores, the cloze mean scores had the highest correlation with both the old and new Dale-Chall factors, .924 with the old and .920 with the new. We decided, therefore, to use the Bormuth cloze mean scores as the criterion for the new Dale-Chall formula.

The new Dale-Chall formula based on the above correlations is:

Dale-Chall cloze = 64 − .95 unfamiliar words[10] − .69 average sentence length[11]

The new Dale-Chall cloze scores range from high (easier) to low (harder), and can best be understood in terms of the percent of deleted words that can be correctly replaced by the readers. Thus a cloze score of 50 would mean that more deletions can be replaced than in a selection with a cloze score of 30, indicating that the passage with the higher cloze score is usually more readable.

The cloze scores were also converted to reading levels, ranging from 1 (approximately first grade reading level) to 16+ (college graduate level). Chapter 2 presents the instructions for obtaining both cloze and reading level scores. The reading levels below 3rd and above 12th grade were extrapolated.

---

[10] Or percent of unfamiliar words.
[11] Or average sentence length for samples shorter than 100 words.

CHAPTER 5

Cross-Validation: The New Dale-Chall Difficulty Levels Compared with Independent Estimates of Difficulty

This chapter presents additional evidence on the validity of the new Dale-Chall formula. We compare the formula's predicted difficulty with the independent difficulty (tested comprehension and/or judged difficulty) on a variety of materials. We were interested in how the formula works on materials other than those used in its standardization.

The Dale-Chall Scores Compared with Tested Difficulty on Standardized Reading Tests

We present, here, comparisons with three standardized reading tests published within the past several years — the Gates-MacGinitie (1989), the DARTTS (Diagnostic Assessments of Reading and Trial Teaching Strategies) by Roswell and Chall (1992), and the National Assessment of Educational Progress (NAEP, 1985).

THE GATES-MACGINITIE READING TEST[1]

We present below two kinds of data on the effectiveness of the new Dale-Chall formula in predicting the comprehension difficulty of the Gates-MacGinitie Reading Test.

Table 5-1 presents the mean Dale-Chall reading levels and cloze scores for each of the Gates-MacGinitie Tests — those at Level 3, 4, 5/6, 7/9 and 10/12[2] — for each of two forms (K and L).

---

[1] We wish to thank Walter MacGinitie for making the new Dale-Chall and Fry scores on the test items available to us.

[2] The numbers refer to the grade or grades for which the tests were designed and are used.

From Table 5-1 we see that the new Dale-Chall reading level scores increase in difficulty as the level of the Gates-MacGinitie test increases. The cloze scores also reflect the difficulty of the tests — with the higher cloze scores associated with the lower levels and the lower cloze scores with the higher levels.

Table 5-2 presents the correlations of the Dale-Chall reading levels and cloze scores with the proportion of correct responses on the different levels of the Gates-MacGinitie — from Level 3 for grade 3 to Level 10/12 for grades 10 to 12. Since the correlations are for a single grade, they are quite satisfactory. They indicate that the Dale-Chall scores — the reading levels and cloze scores — are positively related to the difficulty of the Gates-MacGinitie passages for separate grades as determined by the ability of students to answer the questions correctly.

THE DARTTS (DIAGNOSTIC ASSESSMENTS OF READING AND TRIAL TEACHING STRATEGIES)

Table 5-3 compares the Dale-Chall cloze reading scores with the oral reading scores, qualitative judgments of experienced teachers, and the Spache Readability Formula scores, on the DARTTS.

Table 5-3 indicates that, on the whole, as the selections became more difficult (according to the Dale-Chall cloze and reading levels, the Spache, and the judgment of experienced teachers), they were more difficult to read orally.

Where there was a discrepancy, we sought to explain the possible reasons qualitatively (See the Qualitative Evaluation and Comments column in the table). In the case of *Caricatures, The Farnese Globe*, and *Frankenstein*, we concluded that their difficulty levels were probably overrated by the new Dale-Chall scores and that their "true" difficulty was probably closer to the qualitative evaluations.

Table 5-4 compares the Dale-Chall scores with the difficulty levels on the silent reading passages of the DARTTS. On the whole, the various estimates of difficulty are in agreement — the lower the Cloze scores and the higher the Dale-Chall reading levels, the higher the grade placement on the test, and the higher the qualitative evaluations. The few discrepancies — *You Have Seen Their Faces, The Great Depression*, and *Spiders* — seem to stem from the use of common words to express

Table 5-1: Dale-Chall Reading Levels for Increasing Levels of Gates-MacGinitie

Gates-MacGinitie Test Levels	Mean Dale-Chall Reading Levels			Mean Dale-Chall Cloze Scores		
	Form K	Form L	K and L	Form K	Form L	K and L
Level 3	2.8	2.9	2.9	51.3	51.5	51.4
Level 4	3.4	2.8	3.1	49.5	51.9	50.7
Level 5/6	4.2	4.8	4.5	46.5	44.4	45.4
Level 7/9	6.8	7.4	7.1	37.2	36.5	36.8
Level 10/12	10.0	10.2	10.1	28.1	27.7	27.9

relatively more difficult concepts. Thus, the formula's strong emphasis on vocabulary familiarity seems, in these instances, to have underestimated the difficulty of these passages.

THE NATIONAL ASSESSMENT OF EDUCATIONAL PROGRESS

The National Assessment of Educational Progress has tested samples of American students at ages 8, 11 and 17 from grades 4, 8 and 12 for the past 20 years. For the 1985 testing it presented the results in terms of five proficiency levels — Rudimentary to Advanced. To obtain further evidence of the formula's validity, we applied the new Dale-Chall formula to the passages used by NAEP to illustrate the five proficiency levels.

Table 5-5 presents the Dale-Chall cloze scores and reading levels for the illustrative samples for each of the five proficiency levels on the National Assessment of Educational Progress (NAEP, 1985). We include, also, NAEP's qualitative description for each proficiency level.

Table 5-5 indicates that the new Dale-Chall scores and the proficiency levels of NAEP are in general agreement. The higher the Dale-Chall reading levels (and the lower the cloze scores), the higher the NAEP proficiency levels. Beginning with the NAEP Intermediate Level, the formula levels may be somewhat low. The NAEP Adept and Advanced selections also seem to have lower readability levels than expected from the NAEP descriptions. But here, too, the readability scores fall within the direction expected from the NAEP descriptions.[3] There may be many

Table 5-2: Correlations of Gates-MacGinitie Correct Responses (P Value) with New Dale-Chall Reading Levels and Cloze Scores: Within Separate Grades (N=26 for each grade)

Gates-MacGinitie Test Levels	Dale-Chall Reading Levels and Passage Difficulty	Dale-Chall Cloze Scores and Passage Difficulty
3	-.42	.44
4	-.39	.48
5	-.37	.42
6	-.34	.39
7	-.47	.43
8	-.46	.42
9	-.42	.39
10	-.44	.41
11	-.42	.40
12	-.42	.40

Note: All correlations are significant P<.05

Table 5-3: Comparison of New Dale-Chall Reading Levels and Cloze scores with Reading Level, Qualitative Judgments, and Spache Formula on Oral Reading Passages on DARTTS

	Oral Reading Level on DARTTS	Cloze Score on New Dale-Chall Formula	Reading Level on New Dale-Chall Formula	Level on Spache Formula		Qualitative Evaluation and Comments**
My Cat	1-1	61.24	1	1.1	low 1	Appropriately ranked and graded by word level, sentence structure, and concepts.
Lost in the Big Woods	1-2	59.86	1	1.4	high 1	
The Small Dog	2	57.27	1	1.9	2	
Dreams	3	54.34	2	NA*	3	
Mahalia Jackson	4	50.02	4	NA	4	
Caricatures	5	36.47	7-8	NA	5	
The Nile	6	39.83	5-6	NA	6	
The Farnese Globe	7	23.00	11-12	NA	7	Correctly placed — sentence structure and concepts are more difficult than those found in "The Nile," placed on level 6.
Frankenstein	8	25.08	11-12	NA	8	This is decidedly on a higher level than passage 7, "The Farnese Globe." Difficult words and word combinations: "I beheld the accomplishment of my toils," "The instruments of life," "the rain pattered dismally," "the convulsive motion agitated its limbs" make it appropriate for level 8.
Jazz	9-10	25.85	11-12	NA	9-10	More difficult than passage 8, "Frankenstein," in both sentence structure and phrasing: "The fusion of African and European elements," "its etymology is as obscure as the origins of the music," "bred in humble circumstances," "across cultural, linguistic or political barriers" are samples of phrases that need to be understood for fluent reading.
Work Life and Productivity	11-12	7.30	16	NA	11-12	Difficult words: "specialization," "industrial," "efficacy," "arbitrary," "uniformity." Content taken from mature writing: "Adulthood," edited by Erik Erikson. General structure, concepts and content are appropriate for grades 11-12.

* NA = Not appropriate
** The evaluation of difficulty and the comments were made by highly experienced teachers and reading specialists who read each selection and assessed its difficulty, independent of other estimates.

Table 5-4: Comparison of New Dale-Chall Reading Levels and Cloze Scores with Reading Level, Qualitative Judgments, and Spache Formula on Silent Reading Passages on DARTTS

	Level on DAR	Cloze Score on New Dale-Chall Formula	Reading Level on New Dale-Chall Formula	Level on Spache Formula		Qualitative Evaluation and Comments**
Whales	3	54.94	2	2.4	3	Suitable for designated grades in word level, sentence structure and concepts.
Switzerland	4	45.96	4	2.8	4	
Earthworms	5	43.46	5-6	NA*	5	This is correctly graded as it is more difficult than passage 4, "Switzerland". Difficult words such as "prodigious" and "habitable" can be gotten from context.
You Have Seen Their Faces	6	52.18	3	NA	6	From the standpoint of word level this is not more difficult than passage 5, "Earthworms." But it requires making more inferences. It contains difficult concepts about sharecroppers, their hard lives, what they thought and felt, their worn hands and weary faces, etc. Since this is a comprehension exercise and not for oral reading, it is correctly placed at level 6.
Ralph Bunche	7	36.81	7-8	NA	7	Phrasing, sentence structure, concepts and level of inferential thinking required are suitable for grade 7. Examples of difficult phrases: "pulsating living quality," "kinship for the land," "ancestors had been wrested," "sense of African heritage" make the passage more difficult than passage 6.
The Great Depression	8	42.16	5-6	NA	8	Should present no problems in word recognition at level 8. The subject matter, content and comprehension questions require a higher level of conceptualiza-tion and inferential thinking than passage 7, "Ralph Bunche."
The Maya	9-10	30.16	9-10	NA	9-10	Concepts and word level are suitable for 9-10: "They charted the skies, tracking the course of the planet Venus," etc. Difficult words: "excavations," "archeologist', "anthropologist," "astronomers," "observatories."
Spiders	11-12	33.44	7-8	NA	11-12	Sentence structure, concepts and word level appropriate for 11-12. Difficult words: "arguably," "ingenuity," "ubiquitous," "improbability," "sophisticated," etc

*NA = Not appropriate
** The evaluation of difficulty and the comments were made by a highly experienced teacher who read each selection and assessed its level of difficulty, independent of other estimates.

Table 5-5: NAEP Levels of Proficiency and Dale-Chall Scores

NAEP Levels of Proficiency	New Dale-Chall Cloze Score	New Dale-Chall Reading Level
Rudimentary	55.89	2

Readers who have acquired rudimentary reading skills and strategies can follow brief written directions. They can also select words, phrases, or sentences to describe a simple picture and can interpret simple written clues to identify a common object. Performance at this level suggests the ability to carry out simple, discrete reading tasks.

Basic	51.92	3

Readers who have learned basic comprehension skills and strategies can locate and identify facts from simple informational paragraphs, stories, and news articles. In addition, they can combine ideas and make inferences based on short, uncomplicated passages. Performance at this level suggests the ability to understand specific or sequentially related information.

Intermediate	42.11	5-6

Readers with the ability to use intermediate skills and strategies can search for, locate, and organize the information they find in relatively lengthy passages and can recognize paraphrases of what they have read. They can also make inferences and reach generalizations about main ideas and author's purpose from passages dealing with literature, science, and social studies. Performance at this level suggests the ability to search for specific information, interrelate ideas, and make generalizations.

Adept	37.67	7-8

Readers with adept reading comprehension skills and strategies can understand complicated literary and informational passages, including material about topics they study at school. They can also analyze and integrate less familiar material and provide reactions to and explanations of the text as a whole. Performance at this level suggests the ability to find, understand, summarize, and explain relatively complicated information.

Advanced	26.76	11-12

Readers who use advanced reading skills and strategies can extend and restructure the ideas presented in specialized and complex texts. Examples include scientific materials, literary essays, historical documents, and materials similar to those found in professional and technical working environments. They are also able to understand the links between ideas even when those links are not explicitly stated and to make appropriate generalizations even when the texts lack clear introductions or explanations. Performance at this level suggests the ability to synthesize and learn from specialized reading materials.

reasons for this. One may be that those responsible for the construction of the NAEP Reading Test sought to select passages, even the most difficult ones, within the knowledge and educational experience of most high school seniors. Thus the most difficult passages did not include highly technical and advanced topics of history, science and philosophy, which use a high proportion of difficult, uncommon words. Instead, as in the SAT tests of the 1970s (as compared to those of the 1940s and 1950s), the vocabularies remained not too difficult but the ideas and questions became more difficult. (See in this connection Chall, Conard & Harris, 1977.)

CORRELATIONS OF NEW DALE-CHALL SCORES WITH THE FRY FORMULA

As further evidence for the validity of the new Dale-Chall scores (reading levels and cloze), we present correlations with Fry Scores for each of the Gates-MacGinitie Levels. These correlations would, of course, be expected to be substantial since the early Fry was based on the original Dale-Chall.

From Table 5-6, we see substantial correlations between the scores from the two formulas, and the correlations are higher at the higher Gates-MacGinitie levels. For Gates-MacGinitie Level 10/12, the correlation between the new Dale-Chall and Fry reading levels is very high (.91).

Table 5-6: Correlations of New Dale-Chall and Fry Scores by Gates-MacGinitie Test Levels (N = 26 for each level)

Grade	Correlations of Dale-Chall Reading Levels and Fry Scores	Correlations of Dale-Chall Cloze Scores and Fry Scores
3	.75	-.76
4	.49	-.58
{ 5 6	.70, for level 5/6	-.73, for level 5/6
{ 7 8 9	.78, for level 7/9	-.77, for level 7/9
{ 10 11 12	.91, for level 10/12	-.89, for level 10/12

All correlations are significant P ‹ .01

[3] John Carroll (1987) proposed "as very preliminary and tentative guesses" the following readability levels for the five NAEP proficiency levels: Rudimentary (150), about grade 1.5; Basic (200), about 3.6; Intermediate (250), about 7.2; Adept (300) about the end of grade 12; and Advanced (350) about grade 16 (college senior).

Other Comparisons

The Dale-Chall cloze scores were compared with the average judgments of difficulty by teachers and reading specialists on 50 passages from literature, science and social studies (Chall, Bissex, Conard, & Harris-Sharples, in press). Table 5-7

Table 5-7: Mean Judgments of Difficulty by Teachers and Reading Specialists Compared with Dale-Chall Cloze Scores

Mean Judgment of Passage Difficulty by Teachers and Reading Specialists	Mean Dale-Chall Cloze Scores
1	58 and above
2	54
3	52
4	48
5-6	42
7-8	35
9-10	32
11-12	26
13-15	22
16+	-5

Table 5-8: Equivalent Cloze and Reading Level Scores

Reading Levels	Cloze Scores
1	58 and above
2	57-54
3	53-50
4	49-45
5-6	44-40
7-8	39-34
9-10	33-28
11-12	27-22
13-15	21-16
16+	15-10 and below

presents the results. From it we see that the teachers' mean judgments of difficulty on the 50 selections paralleled the average cloze scores from the new formula.

TWO KINDS OF SCORES: CLOZE AND READING LEVELS

From the various comparisons reported above, we converted cloze scores into reading levels. Table 5-8 presents these "best fits" of cloze and reading levels. The table permits the conversion of cloze into reading levels, and reading levels into a range of cloze scores. For obtaining exact cloze scores, Table 2-1 of Chapter 2 should be used.

The cloze scores range from 58 and above for the easiest passages to 10-15 and below for the most difficult. The Reading Levels range from 1 (average reading level for grade 1) to 16+, average reading level for college graduates.

Both kinds of scores can be used interchangeably, but one or the other may be preferred for specific purposes. Thus, cloze scores may be preferred for research since they permit greater range in scores and a finer differentiation. For reporting differences among texts and of changes in texts, cloze scores may be found more helpful. Cloze may also be preferred for adult reading materials.

Reading level scores, on the other hand, might be preferred by those who seek a more easy-to-understand designation of text difficulty — one that is useful in matching text difficulty to readers' reading ability.

The reading levels cover increasingly broad bands. Reading levels 1 to 4 cover one level each. Beginning with level 5, the reading levels span two and three reading levels (5-6, 7-8, 9-10, 11-12, 13-15, and 16+). These bands are similar to those used in the original Dale-Chall formula. They reflect the reality of the development of reading and of the measurement of readability — that the semantic and syntactic aspects increase at a great rate early and begin to taper off at higher levels.

Section III

The Two Paradigms of Readability Measurement: Theoretical and Practical Issues

*Section III (Chapters 6, 7 and 8) focuses on the two paradigms in readability measurement —
the classic (based on semantic and syntactic factors) and the cognitive-structural (based on
measuring ideas, organization, cohesion, and the like).*

*Chapter 6 treats the classic approaches to readability and discusses their strengths and
weaknesses. Chapter 7 discusses the strengths and weaknesses of the cognitive-structural approaches to text difficulty.*

*Chapter 8 proposes a synthesis of the two approaches. The evidence from research and
from practice of the classic and the cognitive-structural approaches suggest that using both
would contribute to improved results. A synthesis would retain the simplicity of the classic
approach, as well as its strengths in measuring the readability of texts at lower levels of
difficulty. The newer, more complex cognitive-structural approaches would be more useful for
discriminating texts at the upper levels. We have attempted such a combination by adding a
qualitative assessment of cognitive-structural measures to the classic factors of word and
sentence difficulty in the new Dale-Chall formula.*

CHAPTER 6

Classic Readability: Focus on Semantic and Syntactic Factors

Classic readability started around the 1920s in response to two major events of the time. The first was a changing school population, particularly an increase in "first generation" secondary school students. Teachers reported that these students found their textbooks too difficult — textbooks that had been written for high school students who had stronger backgrounds for academic studies. The second factor was the growing use of scientific tools for studying and solving educational problems. One such tool, the first extensive frequency word list of the English language, Thorndike's *Teacher's Word Book*, provided researchers with an objective means for measuring word and text difficulty (1921).

Thus the changing school population — coupled with a growing interest in basing educational policy and practice on objective study rather than on experience alone — gave impetus to the development of various procedures for measuring text difficulty for children and adults, for school and for out-of-school populations.

Several comprehensive reviews of readability are available: Chall (1958, 1974, 1984) and Klare (1963) reviewed the early research and applications of readability. Klare (1974-75) further updated the trends from the 1960s to the 1970s. More recent updates can be found in Chall (1979, 1981, 1984, 1988; Chall & Conard, 1991) and Klare (1984 and 1988).

The Concept of Classic Readability

The concept behind classic readability research has been the quest for greater understanding and for greater accuracy and efficiency in the measurement of text difficulty. The tools that have resulted from this research are known as readability formulas. More than 50 have been published since 1920, but only a few have been in wide use — Spache (1974), Dale-Chall (1948), Flesch (1948), Fry (1968 and 1977), and Bormuth (1969).

A readability formula is an equation which combines those text features that best predict text difficulty. The equation is usually developed by studying the relationship between text features (e.g., words, sentences) and text difficulty (e.g., reading comprehension, reading rate, expert judgment of difficulty).

These formulas are best viewed as tests of the comprehension difficulty of printed materials. They are similar to intelligence and standardized reading tests. Just as intelligence and standardized reading tests assume that the concepts of intelligence and reading are broader than the tests used to measure them, so the concept of readability is broader than any readability formula or procedure developed to measure it.

Dale and Chall (1949) proposed a comprehensive definition of readability as "the sum total (including the interactions) of all those elements within a given piece of printed material that affect the success a group of readers have with it. The success is the extent to which they understand it, read it at an optimal speed, and find it interesting" (p. 1).

Such a definition is concerned not only with the comprehension difficulty of the text, but with its being read at optimal speed and with interest. Although most of the readability formulas in current use do not measure interest directly, some of the early readability researchers were much concerned with the interest factors that appeal to young readers (see Gates, 1930, and Zeller, 1941). It is noteworthy that one of Gates' factors of interest for beginning readers was ease and that the early Flesch formula for adults included interest factors for measuring readability (1943).

Reading comprehension (as measured by different kinds of tests), speed, and reader interest have generally been found to be positively related. Speed of reading is usually positively related to comprehension, as are expert and student judgment of difficulty (Chall & Conard, 1991; Carver, 1990).

Physical features of text, such as size of print, number of words in a paragraph and on a page, and the number of pictures and how they are related to the text have also been found important for a comprehensive estimate of readability. These are still not included in the widely used readability formulas, and hence need to be judged separately.

The concept of classic readability which has been used most widely in research and practice has dealt with text comprehensibility and less often with interest and reading rate. Most of the traditional readability measures have been validated against reader comprehension as determined by a reading comprehension test (Klare, 1984 and 1988).

The Domain of Classic Readability Research

Readability research has been concerned with the relationship between three variables. First, there is the book or passage, which is more or less readable depending upon its internal characteristics: language, organization, and cognitive complexity. The second variable is the reader: his/her reading ability, language, cognition, previous knowledge, interests, and purposes for reading, and the strategies he/she uses. And third, there is the context: whether the reader receives instructional help from a teacher or knowledgeable peers, and the degree and kind of comprehension expected — whether a gist, thorough knowledge, or critical reaction.

Thus, although books, passages or stories can be placed in an order of difficulty based on internal characteristics of the texts, that order of difficulty may change when reader characteristics and reading purposes are taken into account.

Thus, in the final analysis, the readability of a given text for a given reader depends not only on the difficulty of the text, but on characteristics of the reader — the individual's language, reading ability and knowledge of the content. It may differ further by the amount of assistance the reader is given.

What Makes Text Easy or Hard to Read and Comprehend?

Over one hundred factors related to difficulty (e.g., vocabulary, sentences, subject matter, ideas, concepts, text organization, abstractness, appeal, format, and illustrations) have been identified by readability researchers. Of these factors, the two found to be consistently and most strongly associated with comprehensibility in classic readability formulas are *vocabulary difficulty* and *sentence length* (Chall, 1958; Klare, 1963; Lorge, 1939).

Various forms of these two factors are included in most classic readability formulas. The stronger factor of the two is vocabulary, as measured by either word difficulty or word length. *Word difficulty* has been measured in unfamiliar words, hard words, words of low frequency, or abstract words. *Word length* has been measured in syllables per 100 words, number of letters per words, words of three or more syllables, or words of 7 letters or more.

Also related to vocabulary difficulty are *abstract words*, *technical or specialized words*, and *density of ideas and concepts*. All word measures are highly interrelated. Thus, when one is used in a formula, another usually adds little to the overall prediction.

Average sentence length is the second strongest and most widely used measure of difficulty in classic readability formulas. It is closely related to other measures of syntactic difficulty, and therefore only one sentence factor is usually used in a formula. Sentence length is also substantially associated with various measures of vocabulary difficulty.

A vocabulary factor and a sentence factor together predict the comprehension difficulty of written text to a high degree of accuracy. The multiple correlations run from about .7 to .9 with multiple-choice or cloze comprehension tests.

What explains these consistent findings through the years? Most readability researchers have tended to rely on the strong empirical findings to explain the importance of word and sentence factors. Unfortunately, some researchers have interpreted this to mean that traditional readability is lacking in theory (Kemper, 1983; Kintsch & Vipond, 1977). This is misleading.

The traditional formulas work precisely because they are strongly grounded in theory — in the theories of language and reading development. Language development as well as intellectual development have long been understood in terms of their growth with age. The growth in the number of words children know with increasing age, the kinds of words they know, (from high to low frequency words and from concrete to abstract words) and how they define these words, all develop with age and education. Indeed, lists of words known and used by children at different ages look very much like frequency word lists based on their use in print. Thus, the older and more educated the individual, the larger the number of unfamiliar and abstract words she knows and uses (Feifel & Lorge, 1950).

A similar trend is found for syntactic development. Language theory and research has consistently found longer sentences, more complex sentences, larger T-Units[1] and the like used by individuals as they develop (Hunt, 1965). Theory and research on language development underlie the consistent findings on the potency of word and sentence factors in readability measurement.

Also underlying and confirming the word and sentence factors are the theory and research on reading comprehension. From the early 1900s to the present, research on reading has consistently found that vocabulary is the most important factor in reading comprehension. That is, the more extensive the student's vocabulary knowledge, particularly of less familiar words, the higher the level of reading comprehension (Davis, 1972; McKeown & Curtis, 1987; R.L. Thorndike, 1973-74).

Also, the research on intelligence testing finds that a test of vocabulary (word meanings) is consistently the strongest predictor of verbal, abstract intellectual development (Terman & Merrill, 1973; Wechsler, 1974). Indeed, Wechsler recommended that if the entire Verbal Scale cannot be used, the vocabulary subtest of the Wechsler Intelligence Scale could be used in its place. Much of the research on reading comprehension that is based on cognitive theory stresses the positive relation between previous knowledge, vocabulary and reading comprehension (Freebody & Anderson, 1983). Thus, it is no accident that vocabulary difficulty is a strong predictor of text difficulty. Knowledge of words has been a strong measure of child language development, of reading comprehension, and of verbal intelligence.

It is not accidental to find a high relationship between different measures of word difficulty — word frequency, familiarity, concreteness versus abstractness, conceptual difficulty versus ease, general versus technical — and that these word characteristics are further related to word length. (Indeed, many have noted that conceptual difficulty may be basic to all word difficulty — that is, difficult, less common ideas lead to the use of less common words. See Morriss & Holversen, 1938.) That these word characteristics are not "mere surface" factors, as is implied by some researchers of the new readability (see Chapter 7), is explained best by George K. Zipf's (1935) theory of least effort. As noted in chapter 2 (page 5), Zipf demonstrated that for languages in general, there is a positive relationship between word familiarity, frequency, length, and number of meanings. The more frequently a word is used, the easier — and the shorter — it becomes. Words, Zipf said, are like tools. When we want to express an idea, we tend to use a word (a tool) that is near at hand — one that is familiar, usually short, and that has a somewhat different meaning.

The theory behind the high predictive value of sentence length is also explained by the development of language — among preschoolers as well as among elementary and secondary students and adults. The work of Kellog Hunt on T-Units[1] (Hunt, 1965), confirms the strong relationship of sentence length with lan-

---

[1] A T-Unit is "one main clause plus the subordinate clauses attached to or embedded within it" (Hunt, 1965, p.49).

guage development and the high intercorrelations of most sentence factors — whether sentence length, T-Units, sentence complexity, etc.

Thus, the high predictions of word and sentence difficulty, found consistently over the past 70 years in classic readability using different passages and criteria of difficulty, point to a strong theoretical base. Readability research of the past 70 years has tended to use word and sentence factors for predicting text difficulty, not only because they are efficient, but because they have strong theoretical power. See Chapter 7 for further discussion of the theoretical validity of the classic readability formulas.

In spite of the high predictive power of words and sentences, many readability researchers working within the classic paradigm have sought other factors that are currently of interest to cognitive psychologists and linguists (see Chapter 7). See, for example, a scheme for measuring conceptual difficulties not fully accounted for by the word counts (particularly when difficult ideas are discussed in familiar, short words) by Morriss and Holvorsen (1938); and Dolch's (1939) idea density. See also Gray and Leary (1935) and Chall (1958) for other early attempts to measure structural and cognitive factors.

Cloze: An Early Contender to Classic Readability Measurement

In the early 1950s, a strong negative thrust against classic readability came from Taylor (1953). Similar to the cognitive-linguistic criticisms of recent years, he demonstrated that several of the widely used classic readability formulas — Flesch and Dale-Chall — erred in their estimates of difficulty, particularly of well-known literature. Thus, Gertrude Stein, whose works are generally known to be obscure and difficult to understand, had lower readability scores than expected by those who could judge its difficulty.

Taylor's explanation of these anomalies was that for much writing, words are not the best index of text difficulty. It is rather the relationships among the words that matter. These relationships, he proposed, could be determined by the reader's ability to predict words in the text. He demonstrated this by deleting every fifth word from short selections whose readability was also estimated by a readability formula. He found that arranging the selections by the number of words that were correctly filled in gave a better estimate of text difficulty than the readability formula — i.e., it gave a better fit with the accepted notions of difficulty.

Taylor proposed using deletion tests, called *cloze tests*, instead of the traditional readability formulas. He also proposed its use for measuring an individual's comprehension of a selection.

There was much interest in Taylor's scheme when it was first published, and it has produced an enormous literature (Treece, 1992). One may ask, though, to what extent the cloze procedure influenced readability measurement. It is hard to say. One reads from time to time of the use of the cloze procedure to check on the suitability of textbooks for a group of readers. But one seldom reads of its use as a substitute for a readability formula. This can probably be attributed to the fact that cloze departed from perhaps the most useful feature of traditional readability formulas — estimating difficulty *without* relying on testing readers. Instead, cloze requires a panel of readers to judge text difficulty.

What has stood up remarkably well, however, is the use of the cloze procedure for testing reading comprehension in place of multiple-choice comprehension tests. Indeed, it is this particular use of cloze that has had the greater influence on readability research by providing another way of constructing a set of criterion passages of increasing difficulty.

Other Criticisms of Classic Readability Formulas

Criticisms of classic readability from the 1920s to the present have concerned the validity of the formulas for predicting text difficulty, for writing or adapting texts to given levels of difficulty, and for setting standards of difficulty, particularly for school texts.

With regard to the scientific validity of the traditional formulas, we turn to the basic research which has reported multiple correlations from about .7 to .9 — substantial predictions for most psychological and educational tests.

Applications of these formulas to books, magazines, and newspapers have found, for the most part, a high level of prediction when compared to scores on reading comprehension and speed of reading tests. The readability scores have also been highly correlated with the judgments of difficulty by teachers, librarians and students. (For details on these, see Chall, 1958; Chall and Conard, 1991; Dale & Chall, 1948; Klare, 1963, 1974-75, 1984.) Fry (1989) cites additional correlations and successful uses of classic readability measures.

This does not mean that the readability of all kinds of materials will always be predicted adequately by a classic readability measure. Distinctions within a narrow range of difficulty are harder to make than distinctions among wide ranges of difficulty. It will be harder to measure the difficulty of fiction that is highly metaphorical — and almost impossible to estimate the difficulty of poetry. The reading difficulty of metaphorical fiction and poetry is often underestimated by classic readability measures because easy words are often used in a difficult sense.

In 1934 Ojemann noted that, in addition to difficult vocabulary and complex sentence structure, abstractness and incoherence of expression contributed to text difficulty. Ojemann's factors are similar to those studied more recently by the cognitive-linguistic researchers. And similar to recent criticisms of classic readability, he noted that scores would be the same even if the words and sentences were scrambled.

He emphasized that difficulty comes from the ideas rather than from the words and sentences. Difficult passages did contain hard words because the ideas they expressed were difficult, abstract ideas. Easy passages contained familiar words because they dealt with familiar, concrete ideas.

Essentially, Ojemann, as early as 1934, cautioned that readability factors not be viewed mechanically — cautions expressed again and again in the classic readability literature, and more recently by many cognitive psychologists. Thus, although these ideas were not incorporated as factors in the traditional readability formulas, they were part of the broader knowledge in the field, to be taken into account in the judgments of text difficulty.

Using Readability Measures for Writing and Rewriting

Can the classic readability formulas be turned into rules for writing — i.e., can the factors be considered causal as well as correlational? This question has been asked from the beginnings of readability measurement and is still being asked today. Indeed, the concern has intensified over the years as the use of readability has grown.

On the whole, most developers of readability formulas have been cautious and have recommended that the other, broader aspects of readability be included as well as word and sentence factors in writing readable texts. Indeed, guidelines for writing such texts were written by developers of readability formulas and students of readability (see, for example, Flesch, 1974; Dale & Hager, 1950; Gunning, 1952,1968). Most researchers on readability agreed that texts could not be simplified (or made more difficult) merely by lowering or raising the difficulty of the words in sentences.

This caution was expressed eloquently by Ernest Horn in 1937. A noted scholar of language arts and social studies instruction, he reacted negatively to the practice of mechanically substituting easier for harder words to make social studies textbooks more readable. When students were tested on the original as well as on the "easier" versions, their comprehension on the easier versions did not improve. Horn's (1937) explanation was that difficulty in understanding social studies stems more from conceptual difficulties, which may be expressed in easy words. Thus substituting easier for harder words may not cut down on the comprehension difficulty of the text.

Horn cited examples showing how words of high frequency may even cause greater difficulty since the readers may assign wrong meanings to them, and he expressed a strong warning about this practice.

> There is real danger that the mechanical and uncritical use of data on vocabulary will not only affect adversely the production, selection, and use of books but will result in absurdities that will throw research in this field into disrepute. (Horn, 1937, p. 162)

Similar warnings are being expressed today. Davison and Kantor (1982) report that adaptations and revisions of texts by mechanically lowering readability scores can result in less readable text. Also, reduced cohesion may be brought about by mechanically shortening sentences.

Does this mean, then, that classic readability factors have no value in writing readable texts? Not completely. A review of the relevant research from 1920 to 1958 concluded that "while some benefits in terms of increased comprehension and interest have been demonstrated by simplifying vocabulary and sentence structure, such benefits were found only where gross changes were made or when other, more subtle factors such as organization and directness of approach were also changed" (Chall, 1958, p. 166).

Klare (1984), after reviewing the relevant research through 1984, came to essentially the same conclusion. "The selection and use of language variables in producing readable writing has not progressed nearly so far as in predicting readable writing" (p. 717). He cites as reasons the fact that word and sentence variables are not the only contributors to readability. "Among the more obvious missing candidates are organization, format, and illustrations (verbal and pictorial)" (p. 717).

> For these reasons, many writers have warned against making changes in the index variables used in formulas and then expecting comparable changes in reader behavior (comprehension). For example, Pearson and Camperell (1981) remind writers that chopping sentences in half will affect formula scores without necessarily affecting comprehension.
>
> (Klare, 1984, p. 717; see also Pearson, 1974-1975)

Yet there have been successful attempts to help writers use readability principles to make their writing more suitable for their intended readers. The use of guides and manuals which use sentence and word factors as well as cognitive and organizational factors can lead to more comprehensible text (Dale & Hager, 1950; Flesch, 1949, 1974; Gunning, 1952, 1968). These have been used in readability workshops directed by Flesch, Gunning and others for journalists and other writers.

More recently, the classic readability formulas have been incorporated in computer programs for writers. These programs have been designed to help writers attend to trouble spots in their writing. One such early program, *The Writer's Workbench*, was developed by Frase and his associates at Bell Laboratories (Frase, 1980; MacDonald, Frase, Gingrich, & Keenan, 1982) and provided information on the following aspects of writing, some of which come from classic readability formulas: several readability indexes (grade levels), information on the average lengths of words and sentences, distribution of sentence length, grammatical types of sentences used (simple and complex), percentage of verbs in the passive voice, etc.

Another computer writing program (Kincaid, Aagard & O'Hara, 1980; Kincaid, Aagard, O'Hara & Cottrell, 1981), the Computer Readability Editing System (CRES) for writers in the U.S. Navy, provides a readability formula score (grade level and related statistics), flags and lists uncommon words, flags long sentences, and offers the writer simpler and more common options in the text itself alongside the uncommon words and phrases.

Thus, it would appear that the computer has contributed to the use of a more creative, less mechanical use of the classic readability factors for writing. In a sense these computer writing programs are similar to the instructions given in the manuals on readable writing.

What Do Readability Scores Mean? How Are They to be Used?

The classic readability scores have also been criticized with regard to what they represent and how they are to be used to match readers to texts.

The earliest readability measures were used to rank texts in an order of increasing difficulty. This was common practice until Washburne and Vogel (1926) and Vogel and Washburne (1928) converted these to reading grade levels, the levels of reading ability required to read a given book. Thus, when the Washburne-Vogel readability formula was applied to a book, the resulting score was the reading ability generally required to read and understand it. The use of grade level scores became common in subsequent years, particularly when Lorge (1939) first used the McCall-Crabbs Standard Test Lessons in Reading for his criterion passages. These contained short passages with multiple-choice comprehension questions relating to facts, main ideas and inferences. The passages had been graded on the basis of the average standardized reading test scores of students who answered given numbers of questions correctly. Many of the other classic readability formulas have used reading level scores to indicate text difficulty (Lorge, 1939; Flesch, 1948; Dale & Chall, 1948; Fry, 1968). These reading level scores are best understood as grade equivalents on standardized reading tests, not as grades in school.

There is some variation in the use of reading level scores to define readability standards. Most use a criterion of 75 percent correct; others use lower levels of accuracy, at 50 percent. Some use higher levels; Kemper (1983) used a criterion of 100 percent correct.

Some formulas use descriptive categories instead of reading levels. The Flesch formula, for example, uses broad descriptors such as *very easy, easy, standard difficulty*, etc.

When cloze test scores are used, difficulty proceeds from high to low, that is, from easiest to hardest (Bormuth, 1969). Based on the work of Bormuth, a 40 percent accuracy (40 percent of deletions filled in correctly) on a cloze test is comparable to 75 percent correct on a multiple choice comprehension test.

Through the years there have been concerns about the meaning of these scores, particularly the meaning of the reading level scores. In a review of the validation research from 1920 to 1958, Chall (1958) found that the various readability formulas then available were able to arrange materials into broad levels of difficulty corresponding to external measures — i.e., reading comprehension, speed of reading, and judgments of difficulty by teachers and librarians. There was also considerable agreement among the various formulas in assigning relative positions of difficulty, especially when the materials analyzed covered a wide range of difficulty.

Overall, the reading level scores from classic readability formulas that were developed in similar ways gave similar scores on the same passages (Chall, 1958). When the formulas were developed differently, their levels for the same materials tended to be less similar. Those with higher standards of comprehension tended to give lower scores than those based on lower standards (Klare, 1984). This has led to the use of more than one formula in computer programs.

How best to use readability scores to effect an optimal match between texts and readers has also been a problem. Most researchers recommended that readability scores (i.e., reading level scores) match the reading levels of those who will be reading the texts. Since students in the same grade vary in reading ability, it was suggested that textbooks that are used by the entire class have a readability score that matches the average reading ability of the students.

As the use of readability measurement became more common among publishers and textbook adoption committees, and as schools became more concerned that textbooks match the reading abilities of students in a class, the difficulties of textbooks for each of the grades began to decline (Chall, 1958, 1988; Chall & Conard, 1991).

In a study of the influence of textbooks on declining SAT scores, Chall, Conard and Harris (1977) found a decline in readability scores of widely used textbooks from the 1940s through the 1960s and declines in SAT scores following the use of easier textbooks. Thus, the widely held view that the easier textbooks were to be preferred was questioned. Indeed, a further study of textbook difficulty found that when teachers provide instruction, textbooks that are challenging — ones on levels somewhat higher than students' reading levels — produce better results (Chall & Conard, 1991). This was also found in a study of children from low-income families (Chall, Jacobs, & Baldwin, 1990). (See also Hayes, Wolfer, & Wolfe, 1993.)

The Uses of Classic Readability Formulas

In spite of the various concerns and criticisms of the classic readability measures, they have been used ever more widely. Indeed, from about the 1970s, computer software for using as many as five readability formulas on the same materials was on the market. Most textbook adoption committees required that publishers submit the readability scores of the textbooks being considered for adoption. Professional journals in education, business, science, etc., published articles on the readability of widely used instructional materials at all levels — elementary, high school and college.

During the late 1970s and particularly during the 1980s, classic readability formulas began to receive less favorable press. A coming together of many conditions seems to have accounted for the "maligning of readability," as Fry (1989) put it. Although the formulas continued to produce valid results, reading methods textbooks published between 1984 and 1988, as compared to those published earlier, tended to cite the limitations of readability formulas (Chall and Conard, 1991). Indeed, the term *readability* seemed to have dropped from the reading literature, and terms such as *understandability*, *usability*, *interestability*, and *considerate texts* were used instead (Chall & Conard, 1991, p. 76). More recently the word *leveling* has replaced *readability* for estimating the difficulty of literature books for the early grades (DeFord, Lyons & Pinnel, 1991; Clay, 1991).

Teachers' editions of social studies textbooks published in the late 1980s also seemed to avoid the use of the term *readability*. Thus, while the teachers' editions of social studies texts published around 1980 described difficulty in terms of readability, only 3 of 21 of those published after 1984 used the term *readability*. Most of the textbooks published after 1984 wrote of readability in such terms as the following:

> [This book] is written in clear, uncluttered prose. Its easy-to-follow style will heighten student's interest in the material and further their under-standing as well.

> The range of content also allows for great flexibility. There is ample material to challenge students capable of rapid progress. The program also provides experiences that ensure success with less motivated stu-dents.

> Great care has been taken to create a distinctly teachable text, one that will serve the needs of both teachers and students.
>
> (Chall & Conard, 1991, p. 64)

Thus, although the terms have changed, concern for difficulty remained an important issue for publishers and teachers.

At the height of criticism of classic readability, Lexile Theory, a classic readabil-ity measure, was published by a research group in Durham, North Carolina (Stenner, Horabin, Smith & Smith, 1988).

Lexile Theory, a construct theory for reading comprehension, hypothesizes that the comprehensibility of continuous prose is a function of two components: a syntactic component (the demands that comprehending a text places upon verbal short-term memory and the executive control component) and a semantic compo-nent (the familiarity of the words used in the text).

With the use of the two factors of word familiarity and sentence complexity, Lexile Theory brings readability back to the classic tradition. As we noted earlier, these two factors — words and sentences — have been found to be the most predictive of comprehension difficulty from the 1920s to the present and have been the major variables used in the 50 or so classic readability formulas.

Lexile Theory has several unique features. Among these are calibrated scores that represent equal units of difficulty. Also, the same lexile scores are used to measure the difficulty of text and the reading ability of readers.

"Using Lexile Theory, it is possible to construct a scale of the difficulty of 'real world' prose encountered by fourth grade students, high school seniors, or young adults trying to find a job. Test scores can then be expressed as the expected comprehension rate for an individual encountering a text with a given predicted (theoretical) difficulty" (Stenner, Horabin, Smith & Smith, 1988, p. 766).

In contrast to some cognitive-structural readability researchers who claim that multiple-choice, cloze recall and reading rate give different estimates of compre-hension difficulty (see Kintsch & Vipond, 1977), the Lexile researchers say compre-hension is a unidimensional ability that subsumes different types of comprehension (i.e., literal, inferential, author's intent, etc.). They note that one either understands a passage or does not understand it. Lexile theory does not give special consider-ation to *prior knowledge* or *special subject knowledge*. It is hypothesized that such elements are subsumed under the term *frequency component.*

The validity of the formula is quite high — .93, similar to that of the new Dale-Chall formula. Lexile scores also correlate quite well with nine classic readability formulas and with item difficulties on several tests of reading comprehension.

Another recent use of the classic readability paradigm is reported by Carver (1990). Based on his recent research and building on his earlier work on reading comprehension and readability, he reports that "the percent of passage comprehension was found to be a linear function of the relative difficulty of the material. The accuracy of comprehension can be predicted quite precisely from a mathematical equation given knowledge of the level of difficulty of the material and the level of ability of the individual" (p. 405).

For measuring the level of difficulty of the material, Carver suggested the new Degrees of Reading Power (DRP) — a classic readability procedure based on "word length, sentence length, and words on the original Dale list" (Carver, 1985, p. 407).

Carver also reports high agreement between different ways of measuring comprehension — whether based on objective tests or on subjective judgments. These findings are similar to those reported by Chall (1958), Chall and Conard (1991), and Stenner et al. (1988).

Still another classic readability measure was reported by Hayes, Wolfer & Wolf (1993). It used word and sentence factors to estimate the difficulty of all levels of text, including articles appearing in *Nature, Science* and *Scientific American* between 1930 and 1990. According to Hayes, the LEX statistic can be used across the entire range of text difficulty — from children's primers to modern scientific articles. The empirical range of LEX scores is -81 (a primer) to +59 (an article in *Nature*) (personal communication). LEX scores confirmed the judgment of scientists that science articles have become more difficult from 1930 to 1960.

It appears, then, that the classic readability paradigm was used in the development of several new readability measures during the 1980s and early 1990s — measures that presented theoretical evidence as well as statistical evidence of validity.

The classic approach to readability has been the most widely used in measuring text difficulty of languages other than English. See in this connection the comprehensive review by Rabin (1988). For example, Bamberger and Rabin (1984) measured the readability of German text by using both classic readability formulas and "subjective," qualitative measures.

> The checklist of more than 30 items yielded grade levels that could be compared with those given by the formulas. When the combination of the language difficulty and the readability profile was applied to several hundred books in a cross validation, it was demonstrated that in approximately 70 per cent of the cases, the grade level yielded by the profile was similar to that resulting from the use of the formulas (Rabin, 1988, p. 55).

Using the two factors of classic readability — word length and sentence length — Bjornsson (1983) developed a technique, called LEX (*readability index* in Swedish), that could be used to estimate the difficulty of text in several languages.

The readability formula was simply: sentence length + word length. Sentence length, as in most classic formulas, was the number of words per sentence. Word length was the percentage of words with more than 6 letters. The LEX formula was tested on thousands of books and texts in Swedish, Danish, English, French, German and Finnish. It was also tested on several hundred newspapers in eleven languages.

Thus, for languages other than English, it appears that the classic factors of word difficulty (or length) and sentence complexity are predictive of text difficulty. Further, that the text difficulty predicted by these classic measures is highly related to subjective measures and to "readability profiles" composed of such non-linguistic variables as content, organization, print, style and motivation (Rabin, 1988).

CHAPTER 7

The New Readability: Focus on Cognitive and Organizational Factors

Proposals for the new readability began to appear in the middle 1970s. The work of Walter Kintsch and his associates on the cognitive and structural aspects of readability, and Bonnie Meyer's work on organization, were the most prominent. There were earlier attempts to measure these aspects of readability by researchers who worked within the classic paradigm. Ojemann (1934) and Morriss and Holversen (1938), for example, were concerned with conceptual difficulties; Dolch (1939), with idea density. But direct measures of these factors were not included in the major classic readability formulas.

We begin with the new cognitive approaches to readability by Kintsch and his associates — their views on traditional readability as well as their work on cognitive approaches to readability. More than others, his work received almost immediate attention and has had considerable influence on other researchers. In addition, Kintsch's criticisms of classic readability affected the views of many other researchers.

This is followed by a discussion of Susan Kemper's cognitive-based readability formula. The chapter then moves to organizational aspects of readability, with an emphasis on the work of Bonnie Meyer. Some of the works of Bonnie Armbruster and Robert Calfee on text organization are also presented. We conclude with a look at the trends in readability measurement — the classic and the new — from the middle 1980s to the early 1990s, to gain some insights into the views and attitudes held by various researchers toward readability measurement.

In presenting the new readability, we did not attempt to be all-inclusive. Our purpose was to present the major aspects of the new readability, particularly in relation to classic readability.

Kintsch on Classic Readability

Kintsch presented his main ideas on readability in a series of articles written from 1977 to 1981 — his ideas and data on the new readability as well as his views on classic readability.

Throughout these articles, he notes that his intentions are to add to the classic formulas, not to supplant them. Further, he notes that he does not intend to construct a formula "but to suggest a number of different text and reader characteristics" (Kintsch & Vipond, 1977[1], p. 11).

Overall, and particularly in the 1977 article, he is quite critical of classic readability — that it is a-theoretical and is based only on text factors, overlooking the interactive aspects of text difficulty with reader characteristics. He also questioned the value of using the classic readability factors of word difficulty and sentence complexity for determining text difficulty, and especially for writing and editing texts at specified difficulty levels.

We are tempted to respond here to these criticisms, but hesitate lest it be viewed as questioning the cognitive-structural approach. As we noted earlier (see Chapters 1 and 2), cognitive and structural aspects of text difficulty are important next steps which we use in the new Dale-Chall formula. But new measures do not necessarily invalidate old ones. It is in this spirit that we comment here on the position of Kintsch and his associates on classic readability.

If their claim that classic readability is a-theoretical means that it is not grounded in modern cognitive psychology, that is a valid point. Classic readability came into being about 70 years before modern cognitive psychology. But classic readability has perhaps a longer theoretical and research base — that of the development of language and of reading comprehension. This body of knowledge is continuous and consistent from the early 1900s to the present. (See Chapter 6 for a fuller explanation.)

That classic readability cannot be turned directly into rules for writing has been a concern of most developers of classic readability measures. But there is considerable evidence that principles derived from classic readability are useful for writing for specified levels of reading ability (Chall, 1958; Klare, 1984). Indeed, some of the classic readability formulas have been incorporated into computer programs for writing (see, for example, Frase, 1980; MacDonald, Frase, Gingrich & Keenan, 1982; and Chapter 6, this volume). The recent work of Kintsch and his associates suggests that cognitive-based readability is subject to similar weaknesses as the classic measures if turned into rules for writing (Kintsch, Britton, Fletcher, Kintsch, Mennes and Nathan, in press).

The claim that traditional readability is not interactive with reader characteristics is puzzling. The traditional readability measures have used reading levels or qualitative descriptions which have broad meanings regarding what can or cannot be read and understood by different groups of readers (see Chall, 1983; Carver, 1990).

---

[1] We cite from the 1977 manuscript of the paper presented by the authors. It can also be found in published form (1979).

The contention that cloze tests and even multiple choice comprehension tests and reader judgments are not valid as criteria of difficulty is curious. There is considerable evidence that quite similar results are obtained from multiple-choice tests of reading comprehension, cloze tests, judgments of difficulty, and the summaries and reading rate which Kintsch preferred in his early articles. In his recent article, in fact, he reports that similar correlations were found for comprehension based on different tests — that free recall and short answer tests (immediate and delayed) and learning from text are highly related (Kintsch et al., in press; see also Chall, 1958; Chall & Conard, 1991; Stenner, Horabin, Smith & Smith, 1988).

KINTSCH'S READABILITY

Kintsch presents his theory of readability by analyzing four selections that had previously been analyzed by the Flesch formula, cloze, reading rate, etc. His purpose was "to show that texts equated for readability scores may still vary in behavioral measures" (Kintsch & Vipond, 1977, p. 16). Thus, similar to Taylor (1953), he demonstrates that the Flesch scores for one of the four selections was "out of order" with judgment. When Kintsch's predictive variables, based on his "explicit model of the process involved in text comprehension" were used, the order of the four selections was closer to the expected order of difficulty.

The predictor variables used by Kintsch and Vipond included a structured list of propositions, consisting of a predicate with one or more arguments (described below), and the number of different arguments. The idea behind this procedure is that "the meaning of a text is represented by its text base — a structured list of propositions. A proposition consists of a predicate with one or more *arguments*; arguments are *concepts* or propositions themselves. A concept is relayed in the language by a word (or by more than one word if they are synonymous), or sometimes a phrase" (Kintsch & Vipond, 1977, pp. 16-17; authors' italics). What is being dealt with, they note, is "not words at all, but ... abstract concepts" (p. 17).

Overall, the two main factors affecting readability proposed by Kintsch and Vipond are the propositional density of a text and the number of new concepts per proposition. More specifically, the factors included in their analysis were: density of propositions, and the number of different arguments, coherent parts, inferences required to connect a text base, long-term memory searches and reinstatements of propositions into short term memory, and reorganizations required to arrive at the best organized text base. The four passages analyzed by these factors showed a good progression, and in the right order.

Kintsch and Vipond (1977) also applied their scheme to the campaign speeches of Eisenhower and Stevenson, the presidential candidates in 1952. While the popular view then was that the Stevenson speeches were more difficult to understand than Eisenhower's, the Flesch scores were similar for both — between "standard" and "fairly difficult."

Kintsch's analysis found that the Eisenhower speech had a single, coherent network, while the Stevenson speech fell into three separate networks requiring a greater number of inferences and reorganization.

> Thus, our model computations do what the Flesch Reading Ease score couldn't: they discriminate between the two speeches and identify the Eisenhower speech as the more comprehensible. In addition, they suggest why the Stevenson speech is so hard: It is poorly organized, requiring the comprehender to infer connections between parts of the speech that are not stated explicitly. Furthermore, Stevenson's speech is written in such a way that the organization that the comprehender arrives at must be restructured before he can become aware of existing relationships among the various elements. Interestingly, these problems interact with the short-term memory capacity of the reader and are most serious for poor readers. Eisenhower's speech is much better organized, in the sense that our model has fewer problems in constructing a coherent macrostructure for it. (Kintsch and Vipond, 1977, p. 40)

In their conclusion, the authors are quite modest, noting that their analysis of just a few selections proves nothing yet, but that it suggests that a research program to investigate readability within their framework is promising.

They further state that they make no claims to having identified all the factors that make a text easy or hard to read. But their scheme for counting the number of propositions, number of different arguments, the inferences required to connect a text base, as well as the long-term memory searches and reorganizations necessary in its constructions, appear to be important factors.

In a later article, Kintsch (1979) presents the results of other analyses using his cognitive procedures. This time he also uses the classic readability measures of word frequency and sentence length, and finds that these factors were indeed good predictors of readability.

> I do not want to suggest a new readability formula... In our limited set of data the multiple correlation between six predictor variables and reading difficulty (defined here as the number of seconds of reading time per proposition recalled on an immediate test) is a proud .97 (Kintsch & Vipond, 1979, p. 10).

The six predictor variables included the number of reinstatement searches made in processing the paragraph, the average word frequency (a common classic readability factor), the proposition density, the number of inferences, the number of processing cycles, and the number of different arguments in the proposition list. "Most of the variance is accounted for by the first two factors — the number of reinstatements... and the traditional word frequency.... That word frequency and sentence length are related to reading difficulty is not news" (p. 10). Thus, it appears that a new cognitive factor (the number of reinstatements) in combination with a classic factor (word frequency) was the strongest in predicting text difficulty.

The 1980 article by Miller and Kintsch contains an extended and more refined analysis of Kintsch's cognitive approach to readability. It reiterates the notion that readability is an interaction between texts and readers, and that difficulty in reading stems from locating and maintaining relationships between ideas. This is best shown by increased time needed to read the material, by the amount of the material recalled, and the time per unit of information recalled.

The authors strongly believe that recall, which is used in their analyses as a criterion of comprehensibility, is significantly different and better than the more widely used criteria of the traditional readability measures — comprehension questions, cloze, or subjective measures of readability. See in this connection Chall and Conard (1991), Stenner et al. (1988), and Carver (1990), who report that most reading comprehension measures are highly interrelated; see also Kintsch et al. (in press).

Miller and Kintsch (1980) also present the method they used for analyzing paragraphs with the Kintsch readability procedure. The paragraph is first hand-coded into an ordered list of propositions or concepts. Then a computer program performs the next two steps in the hypothesized comprehension process: (1) chunking the text into what are assumed to be reasonable segments, and (2) searching constructs of both short- and long-term memory for already established propositions to which to relate incoming material.

Using this procedure, they analyzed 20 passages from *Reader's Digest* for the number of inferences, arguments, cycles, words per proposition, short-term memory stretches, input and buffer size. The analysis also included independent measures of word frequency, sentence length, and Flesch readability scores, as well as a rating of subjective readability.

Each of 600 college freshmen read four of the 20 passages and was tested immediately for recall and reading time. The multiple correlations of these independent measures were .83 for reading time and .85 for recall.

The predictive power of the classic readability variables is again quite high. "The direction of the correlations... confirm the expectation that low reading times and high recall should be characteristic of texts with common words and short sentences" (p. 347).

In spite of the high correlations (based on the new and the classic measures), the authors beg off any claim to presenting a new readability formula. Instead, the regression equations "should be considered as indications that certain model-dependent predictors, primarily reinstatement and inferences, are indeed important determiners of readability" (p. 348).

These articles were published over a 4-year period. They present an interesting development of the theories and views of Kintsch and his associates. The first article, published in 1977, appears to be quite uncompromising in its criticism of classic readability, although it states several times that the authors wish to add to, not to replace, the classic measures.

By the second and third articles, their position on classic readability seems to soften. In fact, the authors use classic readability factors, compare the results to those from their cognitive variables, and find the classic measures quite potent in comparison to the new factors. By the 1980 article, we read that:

> the readability of a text is determined by the ways that certain text properties — primarily the arrangement of the propositions in the text base, but also the word frequency and sentence length — interact with the reader's processing strategies and resources (Miller and Kintsch, 1980, p. 348).

In a 1981 article, Kintsch and Miller present the most comprehensive view of Kintsch's cognitive model of readability. Although they still treat classic readability with some reservation, they present it in greater detail, thus making it possible for the reader to make his own interpretation. They now acknowledge what the 1977 article strongly questioned: that traditional readability recognized the importance of the reader-text interaction. But they still note that "the absence of a theoretical understanding of this interaction has prevented researchers from incorporating it into their conception of readability" (p. 221). (See Chapter 6, this volume, for a discussion of theoretical bases for classic readability.)

Kintsch and Miller (1981) also note that the classic readability formulas do work and why they work.

> The reason that readability formulas have worked at all is that the factors that make up these formulas are indeed correlated with the conceptual properties of texts: long sentences generally correspond to complex syntactic structures, infrequent words generally refer to complex concepts, and hard texts will generally lead to harder questions about their content (p. 222).

But, they note, this is not enough.

> ...there are no causal — and thus truly predictive relations between these formulas and a text's readability. Hence, their empirical accuracy is limited, and perhaps more important, they are of virtually no use in guiding the composition of texts that are easy to read.... (p. 222).

With regard to the shortcomings of traditional readability for "guiding the composition of texts that are easy to read," it is significant that they make no reference to the research on the uses of readability principles in the writing of readable texts summarized by Chall (1958), and later by Klare (1984). Kintsch and Miller (1981) and Kintsch et al. (in press) discuss the text features that affect comprehension causally, which are similar to those found by Chall (1958) and Klare (1984): structural properties of text and large differences in word and sentence factors.

Since we were not able to locate more recent work by Kintsch, I called him in October, 1992, to inquire whether he had written more recently on readability, and whether he had, by now, developed a readability formula.

As a matter of fact, he said, he had not developed a readability formula. His latest work, in press in 1992, which he kindly sent me, was "A Comprehension-

Based Approach to Learning and Understanding." It reviewed his recent work on reading comprehension and readability.

The paper is concerned with "educational implications of a theory of discourse comprehension in order to illustrate theory development on the one hand and potential applications on the other" (p. 1). Many of the studies cited provide evidence for the effectiveness of the readability factors proposed by Kintsch in his earlier studies. Among these new studies is one that demonstrates the causal nature of at least one of his factors: coherence. When the coherence of a text was improved, large gains were made in the reader's recall and understanding of the text.

Another of the studies explored the difference between remembering the text, i.e., being able to recall and summarize it, and learning from the text, i.e. being able to use the information provided by the text for inferencing and problem solving. This is an important issue in readability measurement and in reading comprehension theory, research and practice.

Data are also presented on the similarities and differences of test scores using different aspects of reading comprehension. Although Kintsch and his associates claimed in earlier studies that there was considerable variation in predictive power when different measures of reading were used, their most recent study found similar correlations for tests of free recall and short answer tests, both immediate and delayed. Indeed, one of the weaknesses of classic readability, according to Kintsch's earlier writings, was its use of short answer tests (multiple choice and cloze) which he claimed were not as good as recall and rate. But his most recent findings seem to be more in line with that of Stenner et al. (1988), Chall and Conard (1991) and Carver (1990).

Perhaps of greatest interest to educators is the study of what happens when "different kinds of readers are confronted with an inconsiderate text — in which the normal coherence relationships are disrupted and in which linguistic cues to the appropriate bridging inference are lacking" (Kintsch et al., in press, p. 23). They found that 6th graders who read materials at a 6th grade level performed better on passages with better micro- and macrostructures. Tenth graders, as expected, outperformed the 6th graders on the same selections, but they were not as affected by the structure of the texts. They read the originals as well as the revised versions. Most surprising to the researchers was that college students wrote better summaries on the poorly written than on the better written text.

> Thus, difficulties with the coherence structure of the text seems to have interfered with the younger readers' comprehension, perhaps because of knowledge deficiencies or because their ability to generate even lower-level bridging inferences was not sufficiently automatic (cf. Perfetti, 1985), or both. In contrast, the poorly organized passages resulted in more constructive effort on the part of the oldest group of students, who responded to the challenge by writing better and more generalized summaries.

> This rather surprising result has some important educational implications which, however, pose a difficult challenge when it comes to

designing appropriate kinds of instruction. On the one hand, less skilled readers and those with little background knowledge in a domain need maximum support. One way to provide this would be to construct very explicit, coherent texts which reduce the amount of gap-filling inferences needed to form a coherent representation of the content... On the other hand, readers with adequate literacy skills who are moderately familiar with the domain might benefit a great deal from having to work harder to get the meaning. By breaking down easy, automatic processing and increasing the amount of active, constructive effort needed to understand a text, learners are forced to engage in more problem-solving activities; these, in turn, may help them achieve a deeper understanding of what they are reading... Students may be better served by an instructional approach that is sensitive to the interactions of text quality and individual differences in readers, but one that helps students do their own thinking, rather than doing it for them (Kintsch et al., in press, p. 24; see Chapter 3, this volume, on matching text difficulty and readers).

We see from the above that the issue of appropriate challenge, that is, the optimal match of reader and text, is central to both readabilities — the classic and the new. While some early critics of classic readability suggested that this issue would be solved by the new readability, we find that this problem exists for the new measures as for the old. (Compare Chall, Conard & Harris, 1977, and Chall & Conard, 1991.)

To sum up the work of Kintsch and his associates on the new readability: Their major objective seems to be the development of a theory of text comprehension — and with such a theory, to explain as fully as possible how readability and comprehension work. They seem to believe this is more essential than developing a practical approach to readability measurement.

Their explanations of readability are compelling and are generally supported by theory and research. But one is also struck by the complexity of their scheme for practical use. And even with this complexity, the authors caution that they cannot, at this time, offer a new readability formula because the most complex of their models is, in their own words, "too simple" and "too stupid." It omits too much. "Indeed, instead of making the model simpler, it needs to be more complex" (Kintsch, 1979, p. 5). "The basic problem is that at the level we have operated so far the model is simply too stupid" (Kintsch, 1979, p. 10).

Although their early articles are strongly critical of classic readability, they do use the main classic readability factors to supplement their cognitive measures. Indeed, in his 6-factor "formula" he notes that "most of the variance is accounted for by the first two factors — the number of reinstatements, as first discussed, and the traditional word frequency" (Kintsch, 1979, p. 10). Further, when both the complex factors and the simple classic readability factors are used to analyze the same texts, the complex measures tend to manifest themselves in the simpler, classic measures of word frequency and sentence length. This can also be found in the research of Kemper that follows.

One is hopeful that their work will lead to the development of improved measures that use their cognitive variables as well as the easy-to-use classic measures.

Susan Kemper

Similar to Kintsch, Susan Kemper (1983) sought to explain text comprehensibility in terms of underlying cognitive processes. She developed a formula, called "inference load", based on three types of causal links: physical states, and stated and inferred mental states. She based her formula on an analysis of 62 passages from the 1979 edition of the McCall-Crabbs Test Lessons, "pseudo-randomly" selected for number of stated actions and physical and mental states. Reading levels of the McCall-Crabbs passages at 100% comprehension were correlated with the densities of both stated and inferred action, physical states, and mental states. As further validation evidence, Kemper analyzed another 18 passages from McCall-Crabbs by her scheme and by the Dale-Chall formula.

Kemper presents correlations of her factors singly and in various combinations. Overall, the correlations of her factors with reading level on 62 McCall-Crabbs passages were positive — a correlation of .63. The two-factor original Dale-Chall formula on 18 McCall-Crabbs passages correlated .64 with reading level.

Kemper's comments on the correlations are of special interest. "Thus," she notes, referring to the Dale-Chall scores,

> sentence length and word familiarity do contribute to the comprehension difficulty of these passages. Nonetheless, when the inferential complexity of the passages is used to predict difficulty, the inference load score correlates significantly, ($r(16)=.63$, $p<.01$), with the reported grade levels. These two different approaches to measuring the grade level difficulty of texts are equivalent in predictive power. Whereas the Dale-Chall formula can be used to predict the readability of texts, the inference load formula explains text comprehensibility in terms of underlying cognitive processes (p. 399).

An additional comparison of Kemper's inference load with classic readability was made on 16 passages from the 1976 editions of the Houghton Mifflin and Scott Foresman basic readers — two passages from each series from the third to the sixth grade levels. The grade levels of the passages, according to the publishers, had been determined by the modified Flesch (1974) and original Dale-Chall (1948) formulas as well as by field tests (p. 399). Kemper found that the inference load scores correlated positively with the readability grade levels: .67 with the Houghton Mifflin readability scores, and .59 with the Scott Foresman (p. 399).

In her concluding remarks Kemper notes again that although traditional readability formulas use only surface aspects of difficulty, "they do succeed in predicting performance on comprehension tests" (p. 399).

The Kemper scheme, similar to Kintsch's approach, takes considerable time and effort to use as compared with the classic readability measures. The recent use of the Kemper inference load in a historical study of American magazines illustrates some of its strengths as well as its weaknesses. Trollinger and Kaestle (1991) sought to find the readability levels of newspapers and magazines read during the 1920s. They asked whether highbrow publications such as *The New York Times* and *Atlantic Monthly* were written at a greater level of difficulty than local newspapers and popular magazines such as the *Saturday Evening Post*.

To judge readability, they looked to the Flesch formula but hesitated since "over the past 15 years, reading researchers have mounted an increasingly heavy attack on the Flesch measuring device and other readability formulas" (p. 208). The Flesch formula was applied to newspapers, and its assessments of difficulty checked quite well with expectations and experience — local papers were easier to read than the *New York Times*. The major surprise was in the assessments of the periodical fiction of the 1920s. They expected a story from the highbrow *Atlantic* to be more difficult than a story from the *Post*. But according to the Flesch formula, the *Saturday Evening Post* story was more difficult to read than the *Atlantic* story. Therefore, they applied one of the newer readability measures: the Young model (1984)[2] — which they soon dropped because it "proved to be expensive and time consuming.... The program is complex; it is a research device, not a pragmatic replacement for a readability formula" (p. 215-26).

They then turned to Kemper's inference load as a more feasible way to explore the readability of the two magazines. Using the Kemper model, "We obtained scores of 2.30 for the *Post* passage and 10.48 for the *Atlantic* passage; according to the Kemper formula, the *Post* prose was written at a second-grade level, whereas the *Atlantic* prose was appropriate only for readers with at least a tenth grade education" (p. 218).

On the next page, we reproduce excerpts from the two stories to illustrate some of the current and enduring problems in readability measurement. Is it sufficient for a formula to estimate relative difficulty? When comparing the Flesch with the Kemper formula scores, it is to be noted that the Kemper is better in assessing relative difficulty, but seems to be weak in estimating actual difficulty, particularly of the *Post* story. It is questionable whether in 1920 or today the *Post* excerpt could be read and understood by individuals with a second-grade reading ability. While the ideas and inferences may be easier than those in the *Atlantic* story, the words and sentences require a considerable proficiency in reading not measured by the Kemper inference load formula. Thus it would appear that, at least for less proficient readers, the words and sentences cannot be ignored. They are not 'surface structures,' as most critics of classic readability seem to like to say. See Chapter 8 for further discussion of this issue.

---

[2] According to Kaestle, Young's work draws on the work of James Miller and Walter Kintsch, "Readability and Recall of Short Prose Passages: A Theoretical Analysis", *Journal of Experimental Psychology*, 6, 1980.

The Play. From "A Prince There Wasn't," by John Peter Toohey, *Saturday Evening Post*, April 3, 1920, pp. 16-17, 124, 127, 130.

The Ganges Princess was the dramatic sensation of a decade. It had been running for a solid year at the huge Henrik Hudson Theater in New York, having weathered a hot summer with hardly a noticeable falling off of receipts. It was Chester Bartlett's first venture into what is technically known as the legitimate field, and he had staged it with that lavish disregard for expense and with that keen sense of the artistic which had given him preeminence as a producer of light musical entertainment.

Written by one of America's most flamboyant playwrights, it told a turgid story of Oriental passion and treachery set against a spectacular background depicting scenes in ancient India. As sheer spectacle it quite transcended anything hitherto attempted in the United States. It presented a series of settings which were so flaming in their color, so permeated with the mystery of the East and so splendid in their suggestion of great size and vast distances that each new revelation was invariably greeted with gasps of amazement from the audience....

Kemper: second grade
Flesch: Difficult level
Dale-Chall: 13-15 Reading Level

The Ghost. From "The Third Window," by Anne Douglas Sedgwick, *Atlantic Monthly*, April 1920, pp. 496-513.

He heard, as he waked next morning, that it was heavily raining. When he looked out, the trees stood still in grey sheets of straightly falling rain. There was no wind.

The mournful, obliterated scene did not oppress him. The weather was all to the good, he thought. He had always liked a rainy day in the country; and ghosts don't walk in the rain. If Malcolm hadn't come in the moonlight, he wouldn't come now. He felt sunken, exhausted, and rather sick; yet his spirits were not bad. He was fit for the encounter with Antonia.

When he went down to the dark dining-room, darker than ever today, he found only one place laid. The maid told him that both the ladies were breakfasting in their rooms. This was unexpected and disconcerting. But he made the best of it, and drank his coffee and ate kedgeree and toast with not too bad an appetite. A little coal-fire had been lighted in the library, and he went in there after breakfast and read the papers and wrote some letters, and the morning passed not too heavily....

Kemper: 10th grade
Flesch: Fairly easy to Easy
Dale-Chall: 5-6 Reading Level

In response to my inquiry about her recent work, Susan Kemper generously sent reprints and preprints of articles concerned with the factors that predict reading difficulty for older adults. In a 1992 paper, "Adults' Reading Comprehension: Effects of Syntactic Complexity and Working Memory" (Norman, Kemper, & Kynette, 1992), she notes that with advancing age, older adults have greater difficulty with working memory and therefore with their ability to process sentences while reading, especially those containing many clauses.

In the paper "Enhancing Older Adults' Reading Comprehension" (Kemper, Jackson, Cheung & Anaguopoulos, in press), she compares the text characteristics that were found difficult by older adults and college students. In general, she found that older adults' reading comprehension and reading rates correlate with syntactic measures and with idea density. Reading comprehension and rate decrease as texts become more complex due to an increase in embedded clauses and propositional density.

Of significance is that these factors, while accounting for 76% of the variance in the comprehension of the older readers, were not related to the comprehension of college students. (Compare Kintsch, above.)

Thus it would appear that when materials are below the reading abilities of readers, the readability variables — whether from classic or new readability schemes — do not seem to affect comprehension. However, when the texts are harder in relation to the abilities of the readers, the readability variables do affect comprehension.

The conclusions were that reading deficits, particularly for older readers, appear to arise from an interaction of reader and text variables, and that syntactically complex and propositionally dense sentences contribute to these deficits.

Similar to the recent paper of Kintsch, Kemper presents evidence on the validity of using text variables for rewriting materials to make them more readable. She revised an extremely difficult sentence containing 63 words, 46 propositions and 5 embedded clauses. This sentence was simplified by lowering the propositional density (repeating important terms and making logical relationships explicit) and by simplifying the amount and type of embedding. She found that those reading the revised version answered the questions correctly, while none who read the original version could do so.[3]

Thus, both Kintsch and Kemper continue to find the new linguistic-cognitive-organizational factors potent in predicting comprehension difficulty. They also find that the factors, when turned into rules for rewriting, can improve text comprehension. It is interesting to note, however, that both Kintsch and Kemper found that their simpler versions improved the comprehension of lower-level or poorer readers, but had little or *negative* effects on better readers — i.e., those who could already comprehend the more difficult version. This seems to bring the new readability to the same discontents as the classic readability. Like classic readability, the new readability runs into difficulties when its cognitive-structures are turned into rules for writing. At the present state of knowledge, it seems that both the new and

---

[3] See Chapter 6 to compare this finding to similar findings from the use of classic readability.

the classic readability are better when used as *general guides* for writing more considerate text. And both are more accurate as guides for rewriting when the original text is very difficult; e.g., Kemper's success in simplifying a 63-word sentence. But when the differences between the original and revised texts are small, the results may be minimal or even opposite from that intended (Kintsch et al., in press; see also Chapter 6, this volume). Compare, in this connection, Davison and Kantor (1982), who note that shortening sentences could lead not to increased but to decreased comprehension.

Readability of Larger Units of Text: Bonnie Meyer

During the middle and late 1970s, another group of researchers were concerned mainly with larger units of text. The researcher who contributed most to this area, and who perhaps had the strongest influence on the work of others, is Bonnie Meyer.

In an article published in 1982, Meyer reports that a communication is vastly more efficient (saves effort) and is more effective (gets better results) if it follows a topical plan instead of being a miscellaneous sequence of sentences or paragraphs.

> That is, people remember more and read faster information which is logically organized with a topical plan than they do when the same information is presented in a disorganized, random fashion.... Thus the plan of a discourse can be considered apart from content, and deserves separate consideration from researchers, as from those who are planning a composition (Meyer, 1982, p. 38).

It is important to note that Meyer speaks of structure as being *separate from*, not *in place of*, other ways of measuring content — e.g., the microanalysis of Kintsch and of Kemper. Her work suggests that the presence of a visible plan for presenting content plays a key role in assessing the comprehension difficulty of text, and that a text displays a hierarchy of content so that some facts (statements, etc.) are superordinate or subordinate to others. Such a hierarchy must be based on a plan, and readers who use a plan different from the author's may be at a disadvantage.

Drawing upon linguistics and rhetoric, she gathered empirical evidence about writing plans: e.g., antecedent/consequence; comparison/contrast; description; response; and time-order. The *antecedent/consequence* plan is devoted to presenting causal relationships like "if/then" in logic. The *comparison* plan presents two opposing viewpoints, giving equal weight to both sides; the *adversative* clearly favors one side over the other. The *description* plan develops a topic by describing its component parts, presenting, for instance, its attributes, specifications or settings. The *response* plan contains some kind of statement followed by a response, such as remark-and-reply, question-and-answer, or problem-and-solution. The *time-order* plan relates events or ideas according to chronology.

Political speeches, she notes, are often of the comparison type, particularly the adversative subtype. Newspaper articles are often of the descriptive type, and scientific papers often use the response type (raising a question or problem and then seeking to give an answer or solution.) History texts frequently use the time-order plan.

Meyer found that better readers tend to use the same plan as the authors of the material they are reading. Further, they remember more of the text on immediate and delayed recall.

Some of her ongoing studies suggest that the descriptive plan is the least effective when people read or listen to text for the purpose of remembering it. The comparison and the antecedent/consequent plans are also better than the descriptive for identical content. There were also big differences in the kinds of information remembered based on the organizational plan of the writing.

Meyer also distinguishes two types of highlighting of information: *subordination* and *signaling*. For example, in subordination, a main idea can be supported with reasons for the reader to believe it. Or a writer may describe an object in ever-greater detail. Signaling is done with explicit markers, such as "on the one hand/or the other hand", "three things must be stressed here", and other expressions indicating how the content is organized.

> Research with various text materials, learners, and tasks generally indicate that content at the top of a hierarchy is better recalled and retained over time than content at the lower levels. The normal order followed in most writing to inform is to present the superordinate materials before the subordinate. Signaling can clarify both hierarchical and semantic relationships. If we encounter "thus," "therefore," "consequently," and the like, we know that the next statement should follow logically from whatever has already been presented. If we see "nevertheless," "still," "all the same," or the like, we must be prepared for a statement that reverses direction. On a larger scale, signaling can indicate how whole blocks of content are related, e.g. as "illustration," "evidence," "further details" or the like. Or a "summary," "conclusion," "preview," or whatever may be announced. It should be expected that signaling operates as a significant aid to clear writing and effective reading" (p. 44).

In Bonnie Meyer's recent work, "Text Processing Variables Predict the Readability of Everyday Documents Read by Older Adults" (in press), she found significant correlations between readability scores (based on her discourse processing analysis) with test items from the ETS Basic Skills Test. She noted that it "suggests that a text processing analysis of test materials may be useful in predicting and accounting for sample response patterns" (p. 25). She notes both the theoretical and practical importance of this finding.

> Theoretically, it suggests that prior research on the dimensions of text readability *are* salient for predicting actual comprehension in *everyday* task materials for older adults... Practically, the text processing model outlined in the present paper presents a useful algorithm for the selection of test items (pp. 25-26).

Both of these findings, Meyer noted, are quite significant. The ability of the discourse factors to predict comprehension of everyday tasks is further confirmation of their broad theoretical and practical value in predicting readability. It also suggests that readability analysis may be used as a measure to predict test item difficulty. At present, most item difficulty is obtained only by pilot testing. (See, in this connection, Chapter 5: Cross-Validation, in which the new Dale-Chall readability scores are correlated with the tested difficulty of items on various standardized reading tests.)

In her summary, Meyer notes that the findings help us understand four related readability issues. First, they provide further evidence that text factors contribute to the readability and comprehensibility of text. Second, "ecologically valid texts," encountered in the everyday world, may be more or less difficult due to their text factors. Third, more difficult texts may be more difficult because they impose higher intellectual/processing demands. Fourth, it may be possible to construct highly comprehensible everyday printed materials which reduce the intellectual demands imposed on the reader. Further, since it is not possible to revise all texts that are beyond the comprehension of older adults, Meyer suggests that

> ... it may be possible to instruct older adults in reading strategies geared to comprehending documents. Strategy training has proved helpful for older adults in both the domain of reading expository texts and performing on intelligence tests. Thus, strategy training focused on reading and using documents successfully may improve older adults' abilities to deal with the documents they encounter in everyday life (p. 29).

We see in Meyer's work a pulling together of what has been sensed about clear and effective writing for thousands of years. Her studies of text comprehension have been concerned mainly with the broader organizational aspects of text. However, her more recent papers have incorporated the findings from classic readability.

BONNIE ARMBRUSTER

Bonnie Armbruster has also been concerned with the larger structural units of readability. For Armbruster, the most important text characteristic for comprehension and learning is *textual coherence*. The more coherent the text, the more likely the reader will be able to construct a coherent cognitive model of the text.

> Texts cohere both globally and locally. *Global coherence* is achieved by text characteristics that facilitate the integration of high-level, important ideas across the entire section, chapter or book. *Local coherence* is achieved by several kinds of simple links of texts that connect ideas together within and between sentences (1984, p. 203).

The basic text structures of Armbruster are parallel to Meyer's five structures — simple listing, comparison/contrast, temporal sequence, cause/effect and problem/solution. Other approaches to defining text are those appropriate for particular content or text genres (e.g. narrative, newspaper article or expository text).

Her evidence for the importance of structure in learning from text comes from the research finding on story grammar: that memory for stories is superior when the structure of a story is clear. When story parts are displaced or deleted, readers not only say the stories are less understandable, but they also do not remember the stories as well. Similar to the findings of Bonnie Meyer, Armbruster found that ninth graders who used the text structure of the author recalled and remembered more than those who did not. Also, those students who were taught the author's text structure dramatically improved their memory for the text.

Armbruster also notes that the use of signaling by the author helps the reader remember (also found by Meyer). Repeated, consistent use of a particular structure in stories also helps readers remember more of the ideas in stories read later since they presumably learn the structure and expect it in later presentations. Overall, "the research indicated that text structure *does* have an important effect on learning" (1984, p. 205). The better organized the text and the more apparent the structure, the higher the probability that the reader will learn from the text.

Content is also important to global coherence. Since content and structure are related, content might be considered an aspect of structure. Thus, information about a character's goal and events that lead up to a goal have a significant effect on comprehension and memory for narratives. "In particular, global coherence is greater when the author establishes a meaningful context for facts that are presented in the text" (p. 205).

Local coherence functions like "a linguistic mortar" to connect ideas in the text. This is achieved by linguistic forms that help carry meaning across phrase, clause, and sentence boundaries. Examples of common cohesive ties are pronoun references (to refer to previously mentioned nouns); substitutions, or replacements of a word or words for a previously mentioned noun phrase, verb phrase or clause; and conjunctions, or connectives. "A rather large body of research has established the importance of cohesive ties in understanding and remembering text" (p. 209).

Research has also indicated that children "prefer to read, are able to read faster, and have better memory for sentences connected by explicit conjunctions, particularly causal connections, than sentences in which the conjunction is left to be inferred — even though the added conjunction increases the grammatical complexity of the sentence" (p. 209).

Why local coherence in the form of strong explicitly cohesive ties is particularly important in textbooks for children is explained by Armbruster as follows:

> Readers try to find a coherent model or interpretation of the text. When an incohesive text makes this difficult, readers spend extra time and cognitive energy to remediate the incohesiveness. They reread the text to search for the link, or they search through their memories to retrieve the connection, or they make an inference about a possible relationship. With this extra effort, mature readers may be able to form a coherent interpretation of the text. Children have less chance for successfully reading such text. They are less likely to know that reread-

ing text and searching memory are appropriate "fix-up" strategies. Children are also less likely than adults to be able to infer connections when coherence breaks down, simply because they have less linguistic and world knowledge to draw upon (p. 209).

Text organization is seen as the supreme source of comprehension difficulty, although Armbruster acknowledges that children may have greater difficulty in inferring connections in texts because they have less language and experience.

Armbruster's recognition that children may have greater difficulties because they have more limited language and prior knowledge brings to mind some of the findings of classic readability that certain measures give better predictions for younger and less mature readers than for more advanced readers. For children or adults who may not have reached the linguistic and knowledge base used in most content area texts, word and sentence factors tend to be excellent predictors of difficulty. For readers who have a considerable vocabulary and knowledge base, the structural measures of Meyer and Armbruster as well as the cognitive measures of Kintsch and Kemper may be better predictors.

ROBERT CALFEE

The early work of Calfee and Curley (1984) also falls within the Bonnie Meyer structural tradition. To Calfee and Curley, text structures are analogous to an outline: the bare bones of the passage. What they propose is that student, teacher, and researcher all need to reach a mutual understanding of the different categories of outlines that are typically found in upper grade textbooks.

> ... selecting and creating the passages for a textbook is best guided by a coherent design. The classroom teacher, in presenting and discussing the meaning of a text, performs best when he has a clear conception of text structure. The researcher, in explaining the processes of comprehension, can generalize his findings most safely as he understands the structure of the domain under investigation (p. 163).

The domain of the early Calfee-Curley investigations is the variety of prose styles employed, often unconsciously, by the skilled author. Referring to Meyer, Calfee and Curley note that the teacher should help the student attain a knowledge of prose structure, but the teacher should also teach the student to recognize poorly written material and to reorganize it into some reasonable structure — and that this helps students become both skilled writers and better comprehenders.

Most children, they write, are familiar with the basic structure of narrative. "It seems equally clear that most children are unfamiliar with the non-narrative forms of prose that are referred to collectively as exposition" (p. 167).

Calfee and Curley (1984) present a taxonomy of discourse based on the work of Bereiter and his colleagues at the Ontario Institute that reflects a developmental orientation that assumes a progression in comprehension strategies from simpler, sequential narration to the most difficult abstract topical exposition:

1. Narrative — fictional and factual
2. Concrete process — descriptive and prescriptive
3. Description — fictional, factual particular, and factual general
4. Concrete topical exposition
5. Line of reasoning — rational narrative, physical and relational cause-and-effect
6. Argument — dialogue, theories and support, reflective essay
7. Abstract topical exposition

Calfee and Curley (1984) present another classification of texts that focuses on expository text, since most school children seem to experience considerable difficulty in making the transition from narrative to expository prose.

> Thus, a simple story is commonplace, a recipe from a cookbook is more formal, and a technical discussion of how deoxyribonucleic acid (DNA) reproduces itself might be classified as very formal, not because of the complexity of the topic but because of the underlying structural constraints in the presentation (p. 176).

Scales

Also during the 1970s, other researchers addressed the qualitative aspects of difficulty by developing assessment scales. These are sets of graded passages that can facilitate judgments of similar text by providing benchmarks for comparison. These include the Rauding scale (Carver, 1975-1976) and the SEER, Singer's Eyeball Estimate of Readability (Singer, 1975). A more recent scale was presented by Chall, Bissex, Conard, and Harris-Sharples (in press).

These scales differ in the number of passages they include and in their content, but they are similar in that the essential component in their use is judgment.

Standardization data from these studies indicate that scales are a valid and reliable means of estimating difficulty; evidence shows a reasonably strong correlation with quantitative measures. They are particularly useful for teachers and writers who need quick, holistic estimates of text difficulty without reliance on counting and weighting text features. It is interesting that this "new" qualitative tool is in actuality a return to the oldest method of evaluating difficulty: subjective judgment. (See Chall & Conard, 1991.)

CHAPTER 8

The Classic and New Readability: A Comparison

Our review of the theory, research, and application of classic and cognitive readability leads us to suggest that a combination of the two paradigms would be a most constructive next step in the measurement of text difficulty.

As we reported in our review of the classic readability paradigm (Chapter 6), there was, from the start, an appreciation for the cognitive and organizational aspects of text difficulty. Many attempts were made to measure these. Because of various limitations, they were not included in the classic readability measures. But they were acknowledged as important. Those working within the new readability paradigm succeeded in measuring various cognitive and organizational factors that eluded the earlier researchers (see Chapter 7).

The cognitive readability researchers took the position that progress in readability assessment would be made by substituting cognitive and structural factors for the semantic and syntactic factors used in classic readability. However, a closer examination of the more recent writings of the cognitive researchers indicates that their readability procedures have incorporated one or both of the classic readability measures. (See Chapters 6 and 7.)

Each paradigm has focused on different theoretical traditions to explicate and validate its procedures. Classic readability has based its work on theories of language development and of reading comprehension. The new readability bases its work on cognitive theory. Both approaches are based on theory — but on different theories.

Where both paradigms are quite similar is in their goals. Both are concerned with theory and with practical applications. However, at the present writing, it would seem that the new readability puts a stronger emphasis on theory than on practical applications. Classic readability, on the other hand, has been more concerned with practical applications.

Both paradigms are concerned with valid and reliable instruments for assessing the reading difficulty of texts. Both are also concerned with reliable and valid procedures for making texts readable for specific groups of readers. In essence, both the classic and the new readability have sought to make their readability factors predictive and causal — i.e., useful for selecting materials and for making them readable.

There have been differences in the factors that each paradigm has used to measure text difficulty. Classic readability has measured aspects of word difficulty and sentence complexity, although it is moving toward organization and cognitive difficulty. The new readability has measured aspects of organization and of ideas — their difficulty and the relationships between them — although it is concerned increasingly with the classic measures of word and sentence difficulty.

There was a tendency by many readability researchers of the new paradigm to play down the word and sentence factors used in classic readability. Yet Kintsch and Vipond (1979) have found that measures of word difficulty and sentence complexity are among the best predictors of text difficulty when compared with cognitive-based factors. Indeed, Kintsch has always written that his new readability research is not to be viewed as replacing classic readability, but as adding to it.

There are differences in the ease of using the classic and new readability measures. Whenever the length of time required to analyze a selection for difficulty is mentioned in the literature, it appears that there is general agreement that the classic measures are easier to use and less time-consuming than the new cognitive-structural measures. It would seem from the reports of Kintsch and of Trollinger and Kaestle (see Chapter 7) that the new procedures take considerably more time than the classic measures. The fact that few applications of cognitive-structural readability were reported in the articles we surveyed in ERIC (written in 1984 to 1994) and discussed later would suggest that they are not widely used. Perhaps it is because they are so complex.

Each of the two paradigms also seems to be better at differentiating materials on different levels of difficulty. Thus, the cognitive and organizational procedures seem to discriminate better among materials requiring greater maturity in reading ability. The classic readability measures seem to work better in discriminating at lower levels of difficulty. Thus, what makes texts harder at the upper levels (from about an 8th grade reading level and higher) is viewed better through the complexity and density of their ideas, how the text is organized, the complexity of the thought processes needed to understand the text, etc. For judging the difficulty of texts for less mature readers, it is more useful to focus on words and sentence complexity, for the less advanced readers are still learning these (Chall, 1983b). Factors of words and sentences seem to differentiate better the difficulty of texts at lower levels. Thus, the omission of a word difficulty factor in the Kemper inference load may have lead to the unlikely prediction that the *Saturday Evening Post* story was on a second grade reading level (Trollinger & Kaestle, 1991).

Overall, the new readability appears to be more concerned with differentiating texts at mature, adult levels. Indeed, most of the examples they use to illustrate the anomalies of classic readability are on upper levels of difficulty. In judging readability of texts for readers who already know how to read quite well, one can expect that they know most of the common, high-frequency words, and that structure and complexity of ideas would be the main sources of their difficulty.

Classic readability has been interested in a fuller range of difficulty, leaning perhaps more toward the lower rather than higher levels. For the lower reading levels, words and sentences seem to be of greater importance in natural writing than the complexity and density of ideas.

The predictive values of the classic and the new procedures are, now, about the same. The correlations of the traditional formulas using only word and sentence factors are now quite high — .92 for the new Dale-Chall formula and .93 for Lexile Theory. The correlation of one of the Kintsch "cognitive formulas" is somewhat higher, .97 (Kintsch & Vipond, 1979). But the Kintsch uses 6 factors, including the traditional word frequency, while the classic Dale-Chall and Lexile formulas use only 2 factors: words and sentences. Thus bringing word and sentence factors together with cognitive and organizational factors may not raise the accuracy of the prediction, but it may help avoid the anomalies found in using only classic or cognitive measures.

It is hoped, also, that a synthesis can bring about a greater simplification in the new readability schemes. At present, the cognitive measures appear to be much too complex, too time-consuming, and too expensive for practical use. (See Trollinger & Kaestle, 1991.) It is important to find simpler ways of measuring the cognitive factors — qualitatively as well as quantitatively.

For all the above reasons, we suggest that future research on text difficulty be undertaken to synthesize the classic and the new readability. Indeed, we have attempted to do so here. The new Dale-Chall readability procedure uses the traditional factors of word familiarity and sentence length. These are supplemented by qualitative assessments of several cognitive and organizational factors. The procedure also assesses reader characteristics to permit a better match between readers and texts.

Classic and Cognitive-Structural Readability from 1984 to 1994

To gain further insight into the current uses of classic and cognitive readability, the entries of the past decade in ERIC under the rubric "readability formulas" were reviewed. Two time periods were included: 1984-1989 and 1990-1994. The rationale for starting with 1984 was that by that time the cognitive approach to readability would have been under discussion long enough to have evolved from theory-building to practical applications. The rubric "readability formulas" was used rather than such broader terms as *text difficulty, readability assessment, comprehension difficulty,* etc., in order to focus on assessment and to keep the number of entries manageable.

During the period 1984 to 1993, ERIC contained 16 entries (nearly 3 per year) on "readability formulas." Of these, twelve were concerned with cognitive readability and four with classic readability.

The main focus of the cognitive readability items was on theory. Few were concerned with practical uses of the cognitive readability procedures for assessing text difficulty or for improving writing. The items on classic readability were concerned mainly with the development and successful use of readability formulas.

On the whole, then, the ERIC entries on "readability formulas" from 1984 to 1989 were more concerned with cognitive readability than with the classic — a concern for cohesion, organization, idea density rather than for semantic or syntactic factors.

From 1990 to 1994 we found a total of 11 ERIC entries under "readability formulas." Of greatest interest is a possible change in focus: About half the entries were concerned with classic readability; another four were concerned with both cognitive and classic; and only one was concerned mainly with cognitive readability.

The items from 1900 to 1994 on classic readability formulas were concerned mainly with their practical uses, particularly for estimating the difficulty of reading materials for readers who had difficulty. For example, Vachon and Haney (1991) estimated the difficulty of science textbooks; Shelby (1992) studied the readability of written documents; Jones (1993) studied home economics textbooks for readers with low literacy skills.

Researchers making use of both classic and cognitive readability studied languages other than English (Agnihotri & Khanna, 1992), health education materials for ESL college students (Bell & Johnson, 1992), and reading materials for older adults (Kemper, 1993).

The 1994 article that was concerned mainly with cognitive readability was by Kintsch (1994) and focused on methods to identify whether a text is suitable for readers with a specific background or knowledge base.

Variations within one decade are really not sufficient for drawing conclusions about change. But it does seem that the classic measures are gaining wider acceptance.

Section IV

READABILITY PRINCIPLES FOR WRITING

Section IV (Chapters 9 and 10) goes beyond the uses of readability formulas for estimating text difficulty.

Chapter 9 focuses on vocabulary and its central importance in assessing readability and in improving the readability and clarity of text. It contains an annotated bibliography of widely known word lists used in research, in assessing text difficulty, and in improving the writing of materials for readers of specified reading ability.

Chapter 10 goes beyond readability measures to suggestions for writing clear and readable prose. Some of the suggestions come from general principles derived from the research on readability. Other suggestions come from a long tradition in literature that aims for simplicity and clarity.

CHAPTER 9

Vocabulary: Its Special Role in Assessing and Improving Readability[1]

Vocabulary is of critical importance in measuring readability — whether in the classic or the new cognitive approaches. (For the classic formulas see Lorge, 1939; Chall, 1958; Klare, 1963 and 1984. For the new, cognitive-based measures, see Miller and Kintsch, 1980, in which they report that word frequency was one of two best predictors of comprehension difficulty, better than many of the new, cognitive measures.)

The vast research on reading development has also found vocabulary knowledge to be the highest predictor of reading comprehension, particularly after the first two grades (Anderson & Freebody, 1981; Davis, 1972; R.L. Thorndike, 1973-74). Vocabulary knowledge has also been the best predictor of verbal intelligence on such individual tests as the Wechsler (1974) and Stanford-Binet (1974), and on various group intelligence tests (Terman & Merrill, 1973). This chapter treats the special role of vocabulary in assessing readability and in developing reading materials. We present, first, a discussion of the vocabulary factor in the new Dale-Chall formula. Second, we review historically the development and uses of widely used word lists. Finally, we present a more general treatment of the uses of vocabulary lists for the assessment of readability and for the development of instructional materials.

The Vocabulary Factor in the New Dale-Chall Formula

The new Dale-Chall formula measures vocabulary difficulty by referring to the new Dale list of 3,000 "familiar" words — words known to at least 80 percent of 4th graders. (See Chapter 2.) Words *not* on the list (following rules) are considered

---

[1] This chapter as well as Chapter 10 was written by Edgar Dale and is based on his personal experiences as well as on relevant research.

"unfamiliar." Generally, these words appear less frequently in print and are more difficult, more technical, more "bookish," more abstract, more literary, and longer than the "familiar" words on the list.

Categorizing words as either "familiar" or "unfamiliar" is a simple and useful way to predict readability. Therefore, we have continued to use it. On the whole it is as accurate and more efficient than a more differentiated classification of words such as frequency level, abstract/concrete, and the like.

It is helpful to make an estimate of whether a word is "familiar" or "unfamiliar." "Unfamiliar" words (those not on the list) are usually "educated" words, probably not known to children in the first three grades and to adults of limited education and reading ability. *Knowing* means that the word can be recognized and its meaning is known. "Familiar" words are usually concrete and common.

Word length is also a good measure of vocabulary difficulty. From the earliest readability research to the present, word length, when measured by number of syllables or letters, or words containing a certain number of letters, have been good predictors of word difficulty. Word length is also highly interrelated with vocabulary difficulty as measured by various vocabulary lists. The Flesch (1943, 1948), Fry (1968), and other formulas use word length as a measure of vocabulary difficulty.

Although word length gives similar predictions of difficulty as word familiarity or frequency, one can learn more from word familiarity or frequency because it is possible to make judgments about the individual words used. Measures of vocabulary familiarity and frequency are also more helpful in making revisions. In a later section, we suggest ways to determine the relative difficulty of individual "unfamiliar" or long words for purposes of writing, editing, and teaching.

For a more sensitive estimate of vocabulary difficulty, particularly for purposes of teaching, a second level of analysis is suggested. The analyst is to judge whether the "unfamiliar" words are essential or not essential for the student's learning from the text. This kind of analysis helps determine whether or not the "unfamiliar" words need to be defined and taught.

A third level of vocabulary analysis is suggested for teachers, writers, editors and curriculum developers: a check of the "unfamiliar" words against a word list that gives the frequency or the grade levels of the words. (See the various word lists below.) This more precise estimate of individual word difficulty is particularly helpful to teachers who wish to teach the important words that are rare or unfamiliar. And writers, editors, and curriculum developers of instructional materials need such information to help them decide which words to define and/or use in explanatory context.

It should be made clear, of course, that no word list or formula tells the writer or editor which words to include or exclude in instructional materials. They tell only the probable level of difficulty of the words. The writer, editor, or teacher must make the judgment as to whether the "unfamiliar" words are suitable for the intended readers and for the purposes for which the materials are to be read. (See Chapters 2 and 3 for additional guidelines.)

The 3,000 word list used in the new Dale-Chall formula serves at least two purposes — as a measure of words that are considered "unfamiliar," and as a tag for those words that may need to be checked further. Thus, the list can help the teacher, editor, and writer decide whether the "unfamiliar" words need further checking, explanation, or teaching.

Vocabulary Lists: A Historical Perspective

Edward L. Thorndike, one of the most eminent psychologists of his time, compiled the first extensive word frequency count of the English language. His first list, *The Teacher's Word Book* (1921), included an analysis of the frequency of appearance of words among 625,000 words from literature for children. The success of this first word book led Thorndike to produce the second *A Teacher's Word Book of the Twenty Thousand Words Found Most Frequently and Widely in General Reading for Children and Young People* (1931). In 1944, Thorndike and Irving Lorge published *The Teacher's Word Book of 30,000 Words*. This list is still used in psychological and educational research and in practice.

Essentially, the Thorndike lists classified words according to their frequency of use in the millions of words in print. The word frequencies were further broken down by suggested grades and age levels — that is, grade levels at which children might be expected to know the words and the grades in which they might be taught.

The value of these frequency lists was marred somewhat by the fact that most of the words had many different meanings — some easier and some harder. For example, in the Thorndike list of 20,000 words (1931), the word *run* had the following different meanings (Dale, 1931a):[2]

> The boys *run* a race.
> The boat *runs* as far as Albany.
> The candidate will *run* for office.
> The motor *runs* smoothly.
> The salmon will *run* soon.
> He may *run* into debt.
> Those colors may *run*.
> The lease *runs* five years.
> The numbers *run* from one to forty.
> The *run* overflowed.
> He made a *run* at billiards.
> There was a *run* on the bank.
> She made a *run* on the piano.
> He built a chicken *run*.
> He is not of the common *run*.
> The piece was molded from *run* metal.

---

[2] The only time I ever saw Thorndike was at his office. I began by saying, "You don't know me. My name is Edgar Dale and I'm from Ohio State University." He reacted quickly and said, "Yes, I do know you. You wrote a sharp criticism of my word list." Thorndike, of course, had already recognized some of the weaknesses I had pointed out, and he wound up by saying if I needed research money, he would help me get it. — Edgar Dale

Many other research studies used the frequency scores in the Thorndike books. One of the best was that of Luella Cole, in *The Teacher's Handbook of Technical Vocabulary* (Public School Publishing Co., 1940). She developed technical vocabularies in thirteen school subjects using the Thorndike frequency scores for each word. The subjects were: Arithmetic, Algebra, Plane Geometry, English Composition, Foreign Language, American Literature, Geography, American History, Hygiene, General Science, Chemistry, Physics, Biology. Two phenomena noted by her are particularly important — that some terms are almost never learned to mastery, and that others may be "learned" at a lower grade level and forgotten by the time students have graduated.

She also concluded from her studies that: 1) some essential technical words (and ideas) are not mastered even by the end of high school; 2) there should be either a better teaching of the concepts or a review in the reading materials to take account of the inadequately developed vocabulary; 3) the rate of learning of these terms varies considerably from one concept to another.

Other technical word lists were developed as early as the 1920s, e.g., *Factual Basis for Curriculum Revision in Arithmetic with Special Reference to Children's Understanding of Business Terms* (Dale, 1929). Of the 2,292 common business terms found, 200 of the most common were tested using a multiple choice test. Later, a list of health terms was developed (Chall & Dale, 1950) and included in "Some Suggestions for Writing Health Materials" (Dale & Hager, 1950).

Irving Lorge, an associate of Thorndike at Columbia University, brought out a list of words classified on a semantic basis, titled *The Semantic Count of the 570 Commonest English Words* (Lorge, 1949).

Arthur Gates used Thorndike's frequency data in the preparation of two word lists. The first was *A Reading Vocabulary for the Primary Grades* (Gates, 1926): a list which divided 1,500 words into three groups of 500 words — the easiest 500, the middle 500, and the least common 500. In 1935 he revised the list and presented a larger list of 1,800 words based on frequency of use.

Dale took words common to the most frequent thousand of Thorndike (*The Teacher's Word Book*, 1921) and compared them with Madeline Horn's list, titled "A Study of the Vocabulary of Children before Entering the First Grade" (M. Horn, 1928). The 769 words common to both lists were published under the title "A Comparison of Two Word Lists" (Dale, 1931b). The 769-word list proved helpful in teaching beginning reading since it was based on both the elements of frequency and importance. Several useful word lists were developed with the 769 words as a base.

The 769-word list was also used in the Lorge readability formula (1939) and later by George Spache for the first edition of his primary-level readability formula (Spache, 1962 and 1974).

Edward W. Dolch (1948) took the Dale list of 769 words and added 231 others obtained by interviewing samples of children early in the first grade, thus making a list of 1,000 words. Dolch then divided these thousand words into eleven major categories including Recreation and Social Life, Clothes, Health and Cleanliness, Body, etc. Under Recreation and Social Life he added these words: *toys, doll, ball-*

room, bicycle, skates, scooter, radio; next he added *circus, clown, parade, picnic, tent, camp, ticket, puzzle, funny.* Under Body he added: *chin, cheek, tooth, teeth, throat, thumb, toe, lap, stomach.* This thousand-word Dolch list was useful for grading early reading materials. (See Dolch, 1948b.)

Clarence Stone also adapted the Dale 769-word list and used it chiefly for the early grades. He took out 173 words and added another 173 words. The added words were easy, childlike words. Later Spache (1962) adopted Stone's revision of the Dale list and found "that estimates based upon it do not vary materially from those found in using Dale's list [of 769 words]" (Spache, 1962, p. 133).

Obviously this 769-word list did not contain enough words to meet the needs of readability measurement at the upper grade levels. Therefore Dale developed a list of about 3,000 words that contained the most frequent words of the English language that were known to 80 percent of students in the 4th grade. This list was used in the original Dale-Chall formula published in 1948 and was able to predict difficulty of selections at 4th grade level and above better than the Dale 769-word list used by Lorge for his formula. Another readability researcher who used the Dale 3,000 was John Bormuth (1966), whose formula was subsequently used in the *Degrees of Reading Power*, College Entrance Examination Board (1980 & later).

Later Dale developed a list of 8,000 words by having children in grades 4, 6, and 8 check long lists of words as known or unknown. This approach had one serious weakness. As noted earlier, frequent words have multiple meanings. For example, the word *game* has about 250 meanings in the *Oxford English Dictionary.* Therefore, he tested several meanings for the common words in the early 8,000-word list and in the later *The Living Word Vocabulary* (Dale & O'Rourke, 1976 and 1981).

Starting in 1939, Dale and various associates began to compile vocabulary studies of particular relevance to education, entitled *Bibliography of Vocabulary Studies.* A total of five editions were published. The first one, with a total of 1,145 entries, was mimeographed and contained 24 categories. The second appeared in 1949 with 1,855 titles. The third edition, revised in 1957, had 2,601 titles. The last published edition was in 1973 with 2,855 entries, 69 categories and an author index.

The final outcome of Dale's research on vocabulary was a book titled *The Living Word Vocabulary* (Dale & O'Rourke, 1976 and 1981). It contains the results of studies of the familiarity of more than 45,000 words to students in grades 4, 6, 8, 10, 12, and college. Separate familiarity scores are given for those words having more than one meaning. The revised edition published in 1981 added two thousand words to the first edition.

Following are some of the most useful word lists developed over the years. They are presented in alphabetic order by author, with brief annotations from the authors.

Annotated Word Lists

1. B.R. Buckingham and E.W. Dolch. *A Combined Word List*. Boston: Ginn & Co., 1936.

    > The authors have been working for some years upon this problem of grade vocabularies.... The first of these steps was a piece of research called the Free-Association Study, involving over 20,000 children and 2,700,000 words of data, and resulting in tentative vocabulary lists for Grades II to VIII. The second step was a combination with this list of the most important vocabulary studies that have been made. The results of these two steps are presented in this volume....
    >
    > ...Ten other word studies were also used....
    >
    > ...Each of the words in the... list is followed by symbols telling upon which of the contributing lists it appeared....
    >
    > ...The results of eleven careful and extensive investigations are here assembled, giving us information as to the grading or the frequency of use of 19,000 words. Of this total, over 10,000 are given grade placement according to children's usage by one or more studies....
    >
    > Figures after the symbols tell in which grade the word was found....
    > (Introduction, pp. 3, 12, 19, 20)

2. John B. Carroll, Peter Davies, and Barry Richman. *Word Frequency Book*. New York: Macmillan, 1971.

    > ...the approach taken was to examine textual samples from published materials to which students are exposed in grades 3 through 9. The publications used... were named by educator-respondents who participated in a survey of schools in November, 1969. Ultimately, more than 5 million words of running text were extracted for analysis from over 1,000 different publications." (Foreword, p. v)
    >
    > The Alphabetical List presents the 86,741 different words... found in the 5,088,721 words of running text... sampled to produce the American Heritage Intermediate Corpus...." (pp. 5-531) Also included is a Rank List, pp. 563-752. (p. 1)

3. Luella Cole (Pressey). *The Teacher's Handbook of Technical Vocabulary*. Public School Publishing Co., Bloomington, IL, 1940.

    > It is with the essential core of terms in thirteen school subjects that... this manual will deal. The first three subjects are mathematical — arithmetic, algebra, and geometry. Then come three that concern language and literature — English composition, foreign language, and American literature. The social sciences — geography and history — follow. Finally come five sciences — hygiene, general science, chemistry, physics,

and biology. In all cases the lists contain only those terms without which the subject-matter cannot be understood.

The research here presented is concerned exclusively with those terms that *every* pupil must learn in order to understand the fundamentals of each subject.

The lists which follow are not intended for use as discoursive reading matter.... The lists are for reference, study, and guidance. They should be taken in small doses, with the addition of concentrated thought. Used in this way, they should be of considerable assistance in centering the teacher's attention on the main concepts of the subject-matter she is teaching." (pp. 5, 14, 26)

4. Edgar Dale and Gerhard Eichholz. *Children's Knowledge of Words*, An Interim Report. Columbus, OH: The Ohio State University, 1960.

This interim report presents familiarity scores on 17,350 words in Grades 4, 6, 8, 10 and 12. The data were secured by a three-choice multiple choice test given to 200 or more pupils in 283 selected schools throughout the United States.

5. Edgar Dale and Joseph O'Rourke. *Techniques of Teaching Vocabulary*. Menlo Park, CA: Benjamin/Cummings Pub. Co., 1971.

See especially:
1. List of Common Prefixes and Derived Words, pp. 326-30.
2. List of Common Suffixes and Derived Words, pp. 331-36.
3. List of Common Roots and Derived Words, pp. 337-60.

6. Edgar Dale and Joseph O'Rourke. *The Living Word Vocabulary*. Chicago, IL: World Book-Childcraft International, 1976, 1981 (revised).
   Includes more than 44,000 items — each identified by a simple *word meaning*.... *It* also presents a percentage score on those words or terms familiar to students in grade levels 4, 6, 8, 10, 12, 13, and 16. Each word familiarity score was obtained by administering a three-choice test to students from schools and colleges throughout the United States. (Preface)

7. Edward W. Dolch. *Problems in Reading*. Champaign, IL: Garrard Press, 1948.

Chapter X, "The First Thousand Words for Children's Reading" (pp. 108-29) includes a topical analysis showing derivation of the first thousand words and an alphabetical list of these words.

8. Arthur I. Gates. *A Reading Vocabulary for the Primary Grades*. Teachers College, Columbia University, 1926.

This booklet gives a list of 1,500 words which have been selected to be suitable for use in all forms of reading materials in Grades 1, 2 and 3....

The words are arranged in three groups, the first, second, and third five hundred respectively. They are numbered consecutively from 1 to 1,500. The number indicates the word's relative position, rank, or order of merit, number 1 being highest. Within each five hundred the words are classified into nouns, verbs, adjectives, adverbs, pronouns, prepositions, conjunctions, and interjections. The same word-form may, therefore, occur several times and with different ranks, because it has different meanings.... (pp. 3, 8)

9. Arthur I. Gates. *A Reading Vocabulary for the Primary Grades*, Revised and Extended, 1935.

This booklet gives a list of 1,811 words which have been selected as highly suitable for use in all forms of reading material in grades 1, 2, and 3 — especially grades 1 and 2.... Unlike the original *Reading Vocabulary for the Primary Grades*, the present list is not divided into parts of speech. ...The words are arranged in two forms: First in an alphabetical list of the 1,811 words followed by a rating of 1, 2, 3, or 4. This rating indicates whether the word falls within the first, second, third, or fourth 500 on the basis of importance as determined by application of the criteria mentioned in the introduction of this booklet. Following this list appears an alphabetical list of all the words in the first 500, a second list of the words in the second 500, a third list of the words in the third 500, and a fourth list containing the 311 words falling within the fourth 500. (pp. 1, 2, 4)

10. Arthur I. Gates. *Spelling Difficulties in 3,876 Words*. Teachers College, Columbia University, 1937.

This monograph includes several types of pertinent data concerning each of 3,876 words commonly taught in spelling courses in American schools. The experimental and statistical work was conducted over a number of years, beginning in 1928. (p. 1)

11. Harry A. Greene. *The New Iowa Spelling Scale*. University of Iowa, Iowa City, 1954.

The vocabulary used in this scale comprises words which have been shown by numerous investigations to be among those most commonly used by adults and children in written communication....

...The 5,507 words comprising the scale are presented in alphabetical order.... The percentages of spelling accuracy are given in each grade for each word which was spelled correctly by as much as one-half of one per cent of the pupils attempting it. The alphabetical listing of the words is designed to facilitate a check of the spelling difficulty of any one of the 5,507 words. (pp. 3, 10)

12. Albert J. Harris and Milton D. Jacobson. *Basic Elementary Reading Vocabularies*. New York: The Macmillan Co., 1972 and 1982.

The main purpose... is to show which words — at each grade level — were widely used in elementary school textbooks in 1970.... The word lists... are based on fourteen series of elementary school textbooks for the first six grades: six basal reader series and two series each in English, social studies, mathematics, and science. (pp. 1, 2)

Total Words, General Vocabulary — 6,866
Total Words, Technical Vocabulary — 7,613

13. Robert L. Hillerich. *A Writing Vocabulary of Elementary Children*. Springfield, IL: Charles C. Thomas, 1978.

Approximately 3,000 pupils in grades one through six participated in this study.... Words were taken from the creative or uncontrolled writing of elementary school children... tabulation, made from samples of writing in grades two through six throughout one school year, resulted in a count of 380,342 running words, of which 648 were specific proper nouns not reported here. A total of 8,925 different words were used by this pupil population.... (Introduction, pp. ix, xi)

14. Ernest Horn. *A Basic Writing Vocabulary*. University of Iowa, Monographs in Education, 1926.

This monograph has four purposes: first, to make available a list of the 10,000 words most often used in the writing done in the United States outside the school; second, to find a summary and a critical evaluation of the various investigations which were utilized in determining the list of words; third, to discuss the most important problems and techniques involved in this type of vocabulary research; and fourth, to show how this list of words may be used not only for practical but also for scientific purposes.... (Foreword, p. 3)

This compilation furnished the most adequate measure of adult writing vocabularies which was available at the time of its completion.... (p. 19)

15. Madeline Horn. *A Study of the Vocabulary of Children Before Entering the First Grade*. Child Study Committee of the International Kindergarten Union, 1928.

The problem was to find the vocabulary of normal children before entering the first grade. Only 2,300 words were chosen for this list although some 7,000 different words were found. However, many of these words occur only once. Words with so low a frequency have low reliability. Because the twenty-fifth hundredth word and ninety-six more had a frequency of seven, 2,596 words are given in this list.

This list of words has three sources:

1. Words children used while attending kindergarten.
2. Words children used when stimulated by pictures.
3. Words children used in the home. (pp. 3, 4)

16. Dale D. Johnson, Alden J. Moe, and James F. Baumann. *The Ginn Word Book for Teachers*. Lexington, MA: Ginn and Company, 1983.

...a basic research tool which indicates the most frequently used English vocabulary as well as those words mastered by about 90 percent of first, second, and third graders. (p. 1)

17. Henry Kucera and W. Nelson Francis. *Computational Analysis of Present-Day American English*. Providence, RI: Brown University Press, 1967.

Comprises two frequency lists of all the words in the 1,014,000-word Corpus. They are coded for processing on IBM and other types of data-processing equipment. The first list is arranged in descending order of frequency of appearance, the second alphabetically. (from jacket and Introduction, p. xviii)

18. Irving Lorge. *The Semantic Count of the 570 Commonest English Words*. Columbia University, Bureau of Publications, 1949.

19. Alden J. Moe, Carol J. Hopkins, and R. Timothy Rush. *The Vocabulary of First-Grade Children*. Springfield, IL: Charles C. Thomas, 1982.

This book is about the oral vocabulary of first-grade children. Specifically, it presents words spoken by over 300 children and collected during a seven-year period. (Preface, p. ix)

In all of the studies conducted, language samples were obtained at different times throughout the first-grade year.... This language provided the 6,412 different words that constitute the vocabulary presented in this book....

Chapter V contains an alphabetical listing of all 6, 412 words. Each word has its frequency of occurrence reported next to it.

Chapter VI presents a frequency listing of all 6,412 words in descending order of occurrence. Each word has its percentage of use listed next to it. (pp. 3, 6)

20. C.K. Ogden. *The Basic Words*. Psyche Miniatures, General Series No. 44. London: Kegan Paul, 1954.

   Contains 850 English words and a set of rules for their use — Basic English.

   C.K. Ogden. *The General Basic English Dictionary*. London: Evans Brothers Limited. First published in 1940; twentieth impression, 1974.

   > *The General Basic English Dictionary* is chiefly for the use of learners of English — for the young who are still making discoveries about their mother-tongue, and even more for those, young and old, who are taking up English as a new language. Using only the 850 words of Basic (which are naturally the key words for dictionary purposes) and the 50 international words which go with them, it gives a knowledge of over 20,000 English words, covering at least 40,000 separate senses and special word-groups.... (Note, p. v)

21. Henry D. Rinsland. *A Basic Vocabulary of Elementary School Children*. New York: The Macmillan Co., 1945.

   > In the fall of 1936 the University of Oklahoma requested a grant of funds from the Works Projects Administration of Oklahoma to carry on an extensive, nationwide study of the words written by children who are in Grades I to VIII. Requests for funds were made on the basis of sampling a minimum of six million running words from at least five hundred schools in all states.
   > The number of individual papers received was more than 200,000, which is about 1 per cent of the approximately twenty million elementary-school children in the United States...
   > ...The present sampling is... the richest from the writings of children and comparable to the largest count from the writings of adults....
   > Of the 25,632 words found in the study, the 14,571 words occurring three or more times in any one grade are given in alphabetical order... (pp. 5, 7, 21)

22. George D. Spache. *Good Reading for Poor Readers*. Champaign, IL: Garrard Press, 1962, 1974 (revised).

   > [See Appendix, pp. 195-207, "The Spache Readability Formula," which includes instructions and list of 1,041 words.]

23. Edward L. Thorndike. *The Teacher's Word Book*. Teachers College, 1921.

   > ...alphabetical list of the 10,000 words which are found to occur most widely in a count of about 625,000 words from literature for children;

about 3,000,000 words from the Bible and English classics; about 300,000 words from elementary-school text books; about 50,000 words from books about cooking, sewing, farming, the trades, and the like; about 90,000 words from the daily newspapers; and about 500,000 words from correspondence. Forty-one different sources were used.

A measure of the range and frequency of each word's occurrence is given by the credit-number following it... This Word Book helps the teacher to decide quickly which treatment is appropriate by telling her just how important any word is... A second practical service of the Word Book is to provide the less experienced teacher with that knowledge both of the importance of words and of their difficulty which the expert teacher has acquired by years of experience with pupils and with books....

A third service to all teachers... is to provide a convenient place to record any useful facts about these words by which teaching can be guided and improved... (Instructions for using *The Teacher's Word Book*, pp, iii-v)

The 10,000 word book was enlarged to 20,000 in 1931 and to 30,000 in 1944. (See Thorndike, Edward L., *The Teacher's Word Book of 20,000 Words*. Teachers College, Columbia University, 1931; and Thorndike & Lorge, *The Teacher's Word Book of 30,000 Words*. Teachers College, Columbia University, 1944.)

Uses and Limitations of Word Lists for Selecting Readable Materials, for Writing, and for Teaching

As noted above, one of the limitations of most frequency and graded word lists for predicting word difficulty is that the various meanings of the common words are not indicated separately. Thus, with the exception of the *Living Word Vocabulary*, the frequency or difficulty of a word is based on its appearance in print. Another limitation is that these lists do not account for the fact that knowing certain key roots might make it easier to learn related words, e.g., if *-nomial* is known, then it will be easier to learn *monomial, binomial, trinomial*. Furthermore, the skillful use of context will often enable the reader to infer the meaning of "hard" words. This has been pointed out by Dale and O'Rourke in *Techniques of Teaching Vocabulary* (1971), and later in the introduction to *The Living Word Vocabulary* (1976 and 1981).

Long word lists, such as the Thorndike and Lorge 30,000, have perhaps had their widest use when their most frequent words were selected for use in other, shorter lists. For books that contain difficult, rare words, a check of these words against the full Thorndike list will help indicate which are indeed rare and need to be explained and reviewed.

Sometimes, too, rare but important words such as *anopheles*, meaning a malaria-producing mosquito, do not appear at all in the Thorndike 30,000 word list. Yet the word relates to events of great historical importance (the building of the Panama

Canal) and also is still currently relevant. The word *anopheles* appears in *The Living Word Vocabulary* and has a score of 40 percent known at the 16th grade level. This is not a criticism of the Thorndike word lists. It illustrates the differences that may occur (particularly at the higher levels) in procedures used to classify words. *The Living Word Vocabulary* is based on tested knowledge; the Thorndike 30,000 word list is based on frequency of use in print.

Students in high school and college should have easy access to glossaries classified by subject matter. They should also know the familiarity test scores of the "hard" words in their school and college publications to help them decide which are important to learn. Further, when a word such as *anorexia* (no appetite for food) contains few apparent internal clues as to its meaning, it should be taught and reviewed. It would be difficult for students to remember the names of most cutting operations, yet they could rather easily remember the root *-ectomy*, meaning "cutting out," and the words in which it is used, such as *appendectomy*, *tonsillectomy*, *adenoidectomy*, *hysterectomy*, and scores of others.

How Many Words Do Children Know?

The research evidence on word knowledge has varied. The estimates of words known by first graders, for example, has varied from about 2,000 to 24, 000. Lorge and Chall (1963) reviewed these studies and concluded that the differences in size come mainly from differences in size of dictionaries sampled, differences in how the words were tested, how a word was defined, and the like. There has been a renewed interest in questions of vocabulary size and growth during the past several decades (see, for example, Anderson & Freebody, 1981; Becker, 1978).

A recent study finds that the typical child begins school with a knowledge of the meanings of about 6,000 words (see Johnson, Moe, & Baumann, 1983). Hence if a first-grader can identify the words in her reader, she will usually know their most common meaning.

Dictionaries of Basic Words

An early attempt to make English comprehensible to those with limited English was C. K. Ogden's *Basic English* (1952). It contained 850 words that covered the "basics" of the English language.

Ogden was not concerned with word frequency. Instead his *Basic English* was devised logically to include a minimum of words that would cover the essentials of the English language for the purposes of communicating with limited English speakers and for the teaching of English. According to Ogden, *The General Basic English Dictionary* was devised for the use of learners of English — the young who are still learning their mother-tongue, and even more, for those, young and old, who are taking up English as a new language.

Michael West and James Gareth Endicott used a list of 1,490 simple words to define all words in their *The New Method English Dictionary* (1961). Similar to Ogden, they were interested in preparing instructional materials for those who were first

Table 9-1: A Comparison of Definitions from Ogden's *Basic English* (1952) and West and Endicott's *New Method English Dictionary* (1961)

	Ogden	**West**
govern	be ruling, in control of	to direct or control or rule
health	condition of body	state of being well
ice	water made solid by cold	water that has become solid with cold
magniloquent	high-sounding, over-important	speaking in a foolishly solemn way
premonition	feeling taken as sign of coming event	a feeling that a certain event is going to happen
mosaic	(Form, work, or art), in which designs are produced by joining bits of glass, stone, etc., of different colours	picture made up of small pieces of coloured glass or stone
run	go on foot at rate quicker than walking; go quickly; do regular journey; walled place for animals	act of moving quickly; move or travel; enclosed place for animals

learning English, especially the foreign-born.

The New Method English Dictionary (1961) was in its 5th edition in 1976. It defined over 24,000 items — some 18,000 words and 8,000 idioms. Strangely enough, West did not make the claim, as he could have, that this dictionary was especially valuable for readers of English who wanted simple, readable definitions. Note, in Table 9-1, the definitions given for the same words by Ogden and by West.

The defining of harder words with easier ones has been a goal of children's dictionaries for many decades. Such dictionaries define hard words with simpler ones. (See the *Thorndike-Barnhart Dictionary*: Barnhart, 1952.)

The Original and the New Dale List of 3,000 Words

The original Dale list of 3,000 words was based on the words passed by 80 percent of 4th graders on a judgment test. The words were also checked against the grade level scores on Arthur Gates' *Spelling Difficulties in 3,876 Words* (Columbia University, 1937).

The new Dale 3,000-word list is based on familiarity scores from *The Living Word Vocabulary* (Dale & O'Rourke, 1981). Those words known by at least 80 percent of 4th graders were included in the new 3,000. The new list contains a greater number of scientific and technical words such as *channel, capsule, blastoff*[3]. These did not appear on the original 3,000. On the whole, the words added to the new Dale list of 3,000 words tended to be technical, scientific, and abstract.

Words dropped from the original list in preparing the new 3,000 tended to be

---

[3] Although the new 3,000 list does not include familiarity scores for multiple meanings, each of the words was tested for multiple meanings. These are reported in *The Living Word Vocabulary*, 1981.

rural and farm words (such as *cackle, cluck, manger,* and *stump) and* words that seemed "dated," such as *clump, christen, hark, rosebud, trolley.*

The additions and deletions from the old to the new list tended to reflect the changes over the past four decades in our life and culture — from an agricultural and more concrete world to one that is more scientific, technical and abstract.

Additional changes:

- We excluded as separate items in the new 3,000 list many compound and hyphenated words whose separate components were at the 4th grade level, and therefore would be counted as familiar: *billboard, candlestick, gingerbread,* and *schoolhouse.*
- In the original 3,000, inflected words were listed separately. In the new list they are grouped and listed together as follows:

    bake (r) (ry);
    cheer (ful) (y);
    collect (ion) (or);
    fat (ter) (test);
    big (ger) (ness).

Summary

We have presented an introduction to the existing word lists to assist the researcher and the writer in estimating text difficulty and in writing more readable text. Other issues relevant to the use of vocabulary lists such as the number of words known by children of different ages and grades and the change in familiarity of words are also discussed.

CHAPTER 10

Creating Readable Materials: Writing and Editing

This chapter is concerned with how readability principles may be used to write and edit materials suitable for readers of a given level of proficiency. As indicated in previous chapters, classic readability formulas have their major use in predicting the reading difficulty of a text, i.e., the level of reading ability generally needed to read and understand it. Using readability formulas to write or edit to a specific level of difficulty is less effective. The existing research evidence suggests that small changes made by substituting easier for harder words and shorter for longer sentences may not always improve comprehension. However, it does suggest that when extensive changes in words and sentences are made, readability may be effected positively. But of even greater power are changes in words and sentences along with changes made in structure and organization, in concept difficulty, and in interest appeal. (See Chapters 6 & 7; Chall, 1958; Klare, 1984).

The techniques for writing and editing suggested here come from readability research and also from techniques long known in journalism and in literature, such as those suggested by Strunk and White (1978). These are techniques that alert the writer and editor to improving the difficulty and clarity of text, irrespective of readability scores.

It is helpful to think of the kind of materials that benefit from improved readability — materials written for a mass audience, such as tax forms, voting instructions, patent medicine inserts, and instructions for constructing furniture or toys. Such written materials are best done when they can be read by those with limited reading ability as well as by skilled readers. Much advertising material would fall into this category. The major purpose of such written material is to inform widely and effectively. These materials need to be as readable as the topic and information to be conveyed permit, and they need to be written as clearly as possible.

A second type of text that needs to be readable and clear is instructional materials in different content areas for elementary and secondary students who read at different levels of maturity and complexity. Such material is generally written with a certain level of reading proficiency in mind, and readability measures can help the writer and editor estimate whether the text "matches" the students' level of proficiency. If the readability level is above or below the readers' proficiency, adjustments can be made. Again, the existing research indicates that this can best be done not by mechanically increasing or decreasing the unfamiliar word and sentence counts, but by concern for concept difficulty, reader interest, and text coherence. (See Chapter 3 for criteria regarding optimal levels of difficulty.)

To use readability measures effectively, it is therefore necessary to ask before one writes or edits: Who will read this article or book? What is their average reading ability? Is it intended for all adults in the United States? Is the targeted audience a more specialized one, such as food-stamp users? If the material is for a school audience, it is useful to know what grade. If the material is for college, it helps to know whether it is targeted for specialists or non-specialists.

The first step, then, is to form a mental picture of the prospective readers, then to try to determine what is to be conveyed to them through *their* eyes and *their* thought processes. For example, in a national campaign to improve the writing of journalists, Rudolf Flesch pointed out the reading abilities and distractions of average readers:

> AP stories are written for newspaper readers, radio and television listeners. That means you are writing for someone who spends half an hour, more or less, on the daily paper, reading some of the stories, glancing at others, and skipping most. Or someone who listens to a five- or fifteen-minute newscast, sometimes giving it only part of his attention.
>
> Newspaper readers read fairly slowly — maybe 200 words a minute — paying only casual attention to what they read. More often than not, they read the paper against a background of noise and interruptions. Their fund of information is meager...their familiarity with current news is shaky... (Flesch, 1951, p. 2)

A key consideration in developing written materials is knowing the reading level of the intended audience. A recent survey of reading ability by the National Assessment of Educational Progress (NAEP) (1985) found that about 40 percent of young adults of 17 to 25 and no longer in school, and 17 year olds in high school, read at an "adept" level. Sixty percent read at a lower level. An "adept" level is equivalent to about a 12th grade reading level. The percentage who can read on an "adept" level drops to 10-20 percent for those classified as minority or low socio-economic level.

If no other information about the reading level of an intended audience is available, one can use the last grade reached in school or college. The last grade reached roughly corresponds with a person's reading level, although the NAEP test results cited earlier suggest that the last grade reached may be higher than tested reading ability. The recent estimates from NAEP noted above are that only about 40 percent of young adults are able to read 12th grade material, although about 75 percent complete 12th grade.

Reading level, it should be remembered, does not mean intelligence level. Adults with high intelligence may not have attended school long enough to acquire a high level of literacy, or they may have a reading or learning disability, or they may have encountered other obstacles to acquiring reading proficiency.

When material is classified as 6th grade reading level, one should not assume that it fits *only* readers with 6th grade reading ability. More accurately, it means that the book or pamphlet can be read and understood by readers at 6th grade reading ability and higher.

Writers who prepare newsletters or news magazines for all of the members of large corporations may find that their employees include personnel with Ph.D.'s as well as workers who have not completed high school. It is important, therefore, that the range of reading ability levels also be considered. For example, articles on company safety rules that are to be read and understood by all employees and management might be written at about a 7th grade reading level so that the material is understandable for almost everyone.

It is important to get feedback concerning the effectiveness of an article, a chapter, or a book. In writing for a multilevel audience it is vital to try out the article or story on representative readers to determine if it is on target, and which information is too easy or too difficult.

Other questions should be asked about the audience. Where will the materials be read? Will the audience be reading "on the run," or will they have a chance to study the information carefully and thoughtfully? Will the readers be reading independently, or will they be in a classroom and have access to teachers or fellow students for commentary and help?

Reader Interest

Many newsletters or pamphlets are read in a doctor's office, at a bus station, or in an airplane. The author must be brief. He is writing for a reader-in-a-hurry. The writer of well-written informational material for an audience on-the-run does not waste time getting to the point. The article must move briskly with no wasted motion.

Vivid visual and verbal cues also help to catch the interest of the inattentive reader. Well-mapped, carefully organized writing keeps a reader from giving up on an article.

If readers are involved in classroom study, they have the benefit of a teacher and classmates to amplify and qualify explanations and information. If readers are studying materials independently, self-help aids must be built in. A glossary of technical terms (tied closely to the material in which the words are used), contextual explanations for hard words and ideas, and a summary at the end of each section are helpful.

It helps a writer to know the approximate age of the intended audience. If the writing is for young readers, remember that some information that is first-hand to the writer may really be unknown to them. For example, today's college students have no first-hand experience with any events, fads, and trends that took place in the sixties. Pictures and words must be used in order to help a young audience see where an event in 1950 took place, what an important leader of the 1940s looked like, how he acted or reacted.

Reading audiences in schools and colleges should be distinguished from more general audiences. The reading material that students use (particularly in elementary and high school) is intended both for their instruction and also for improving their reading skills (Chall & Conard, 1991; see Chapter 3). For a school and college audience, then, one must be concerned not only with the audience's understanding but that the difficulty of the material is optimal for their reading development — not too easy or too hard.

When you are ready to write, you will need also to think about the nature of the information you are to impart. Are the ideas abstract or concrete? A concrete idea is one that can be sensed, touched, pointed to, or tasted. It has an existence in time and space. An abstraction, on the other hand, is something you cannot see even if you are looking right at it. It is intangible, untouchable, immaterial. Concepts like *charity*, *zero*, and *pragmatism* are abstract. Their meaning is not readily apparent, but must be worked out, discovered.

Abstract ideas are difficult; therefore, it is helpful to use concrete examples to clarify the abstract ideas. It is not difficult for a writer to see and describe the seed in the apple. It requires creative imagination, however, to introduce the reader to the abstract concept of the apple in the seed. Thumb through a copy of the *Reader's Digest* and note how often concrete examples and quotations are used to make abstract ideas less difficult.

The able writer realizes that ideas can be placed on a scale, a continuum. On the easy end are nontechnical, personal, and concrete ideas. On the difficult end of the scale are technical, impersonal, and abstract ideas. Complex ideas cannot always be made simple, but they can be made comprehensible by adding concrete examples.

One way to make abstract ideas understandable is to "examplify" them. To "examplify" means to *amplify by example*. *Archaeology*, the study of the old, is an abstract concept. However, it can be made understandable to children when examples are given.

If the subject of your material is abstract, you must creatively expand your concepts. You may need to explain a hard idea several times — each time using a slightly different approach, a different example. The use of appropriate graphics — photographs, charts, graphs — can also help a reader work through the intellectual maze.

How long will your material be? Do you plan to present many ideas? If so, you may want to divide your information into appropriate segments, chapters, sections. If you have too many ideas to be digested in a single reading, plan for appropriate stopping places, for breathers. For example, an anecdote may be needed to provide a refreshing pause.

Check the length of your chapters. Do they require too much concentration over a long period of time? Too many closely packed ideas may mean that your readers will quit reading before they finish the chapter.

What do you expect readers to do with the material? Are they merely to put it into their own words, using only limited evaluation and inference? If so, you are asking for the use of *lower mental processes*. If you expect readers to read the material, translate it, draw inferences, make critical judgments, and then apply what has been read to their own problems, you are requiring the use of *higher mental processes*. When the ideas become the reader's, you have *implication* and *application*.

To write for implication and application, you will encourage the reader to "talk back" to the printed page. You may want to insert questions into the material, to ask from time to time, "What do *you* think?" Skillful questions and suggested activities at the end of the chapter may stimulate readers to read between and beyond the lines.

Once you have pinpointed your intended audience and your purpose, you need to evaluate what you have written. Some appropriate questions are:

1. What is its readability level? Does it match the reading levels of the expected readers? (See Chapter 3 for optimal matching.)
2. Are my main ideas and points abstract or concrete?
3. How much material has been included?
4. Have I divided my material into segments of appropriate length? Do some of my chapters or sections require too much concentration over too long a period of time?
5. Does my material require reader application?

Clear, Concise Writing

A good writer, like a good teacher, is sympathetic and explains well. Good writing involves the use of feelings as well as of intellect. Well-written material at all levels of difficulty is sympathetic and shares ideas and feelings in a mood of mutuality. It is a two-way sharing process. It should be inter-communication because it is the action and interaction of minds that educate.

Effective writing is clear. Louis M. Lyons (1965, p. 296), the late reporter and editor of the *Nieman Reports*, once said that the opposite of clarity is obscurity:

> Journalists have a word for it — fog — which means just what it says. Fog gets in the way of clear, definite statements. It has to be rigorously edited out and the sentences thinned down and straightened out to say what it means to say without any fuss or blur or uncertainty.

Clear writing is like clear broth: all the fat and extraneous materials have been strained out. The reader doesn't have to cope with unimportant details, irrelevant facts, illogical meanderings.[1] The writer avoids meaningless wordage sometimes called *gobbledygook*. Gobbledygook is written or spoken speech that is hard to understand because of overuse of vague abstractions and involved sentences.

---

[1] You may want to study such classics about simple writing as the following:
Barzun, Jacques (1975). *Simple and direct, A rhetoric for writers*. New York: Harper and Row.
Gunning, Robert (1968). *The technique of clear writing* (revised ed). New York: McGraw-Hill.

Examples of gobbledygook include: "he proceeded on the assumption" instead of "he assumed," or "many of our big cities are confronted by financial problems of enormous magnitude" instead of "many of our big cities are broke."

Following are some simple ways to slim down "fat" phrases found in articles, themes, theses, and other writing:

1. *Simplify the sentence by using an active instead of a passive verb.*

Original	*Revised Version*
has made an attempt	has tried
had been a deterrent to	had hindered
have been making studies of	have studied

2. *Avoid unnecessary use of make, made, making.*

they made an attempt	they tried
made it possible for	enabled
make a careful analysis	analyze carefully

3. *Substitute a single word for a phrase.*

a good deal of	much
a large portion of	most
a great majority of	most
the vast majority	most

4. *Eliminate trite phrases.*

cessation of hostilities	end of the war
endeavor to ascertain	try to find out
This meets with our approval	We approve

5. *Substitute gerunds for noun phrases — shun the -tion words.*

the introduction of	introducing
the reception of	receiving
the reduction of	reducing
the utilization of	using

6. *Avoid overuse of "it is…"*

It is possible that	possibly
It is anticipated that	we anticipate
It is highly probable that	probably
It is my conviction that	I am convinced

7. *Reduce long, complicated phrases.*

are not able to	cannot
direct your inquiries to	write to
experience has indicated that	we learned that
exploited to the fullest extent	fully exploited
At this point in time	now

8. *Simplify prepositional phrases.*

at all times	always
at the present time	now
in the amount of $10.00	for $10.00
in the development of	in developing
in the meantime	meanwhile
to the attainment of	to attain
through the use of	by using

9. *Eliminate unnecessary words.*

aware of the fact that	aware that
if it is deemed satisfactory	if satisfactory
in the course of his speech	in his speech

Certain phrases and expressions grow stale because of overuse. The effective phrase, the clever expression, may be repeated so many times that it becomes a cliché. Some expressions used widely during the past two decades include *firm up, finalize, early on, facet, generation gap, life-style, paradigm, scenario, viable, bottom line, savaged, meaningful relationship.* Some of these expressions may remain useful; others will drop out.

Vocabulary

Effective writing for a wide audience should be no harder than it needs to be. A good writer does not use big words when little ones will do. John Dryden, English poet and critic, noted that too often writers "dress pygmy thoughts in giant words."

When a technical or difficult word is needed, however, the writer should use it, especially in materials meant to inform and instruct. In fact, technical vocabulary must be used in contracts, in tax instructions, in financial information. If you are preparing an article on auto mechanics, you cannot refer to the alternator as a "thingamabob," or the connecting rod as a "whatchamacallit." Einstein's statement that "Everything must be made as simple as possible, but not one bit simpler" applies here. You cannot avoid hard concepts, and you cannot skip important, technical terms that are difficult.

You can help readers understand these words, however, by defining or using them in a context that explains the meaning. Hard ideas can be made understandable by providing many interesting, lively examples. You can introduce hard technical terms by defining them, by using them in context, and by providing a glossary.

Much of the difficulty in reading is caused by unknown vocabulary. Beyond a 4th grade reading level materials begin to contain abstract, technical, and literary words. Some of these words are never thoroughly learned by the average adult. Their meanings remain vague. Thus, a clear understanding of what is read depends either on limiting or explaining these words.

To know which technical terms are known or unknown by readers of different educational levels, consult the new Dale list in Chapter 2 and the Dale and O'Rourke *The Living Word Vocabulary* (1976 and 1981), or some other source. If the word is known by fewer than one-half of your audience, you should define it directly or contextually.

Readers can be encouraged to review technical word meanings if easy-to-use glossaries are provided. Should a glossary appear at the end of the book, or should it be used at the end — or beginning — of each chapter? If chapters are long, should several glossaries be included at appropriate places?

A glossary has several advantages when it is presented by chapters or by units of instruction. It makes clear that the technical terms noted are important goals of instruction. It may also show authors that various sections of their material are overloaded with hard, technical terms. For example, if readers are studying figures of speech, they may not know *oxymoron, alliteration, simile, metaphor, metonymy, euphemism, synecdoche*. Further, important glossary terms can be repeated in later chapters.

Another approach to easing the problem of technical vocabulary is to use italics. This gives readers a signal.

But first, a word of caution must be stated. When you select definitions for technical words, be sure that your definitions are clear. Some definitions are so complete and scholarly that they are difficult for students or nonspecialists to understand. If you fill your glossary with such definitions, you will lose your reader. Here, for example, is a complex definition of the word *door*:

> A movable piece of firm material or a structure supported usually along one side and swinging on pivots or hinges, sliding along a groove, rolling up and down, revolving as one of four leaves, or folding like an accordion by means of which an opening may be closed or kept open for passage into or out of a building, room or other covered enclosure of car, airplane, elevator, or other vehicle. (Gove [Ed.], *Webster's Third New International Dictionary of the English Language, Unabridged*, 1961, p. 674)

Another way to help your reader understand difficult, technical terms and ideas is to place the words and ideas in a meaningful context. Actually the process of education is one of learning how to contextualize one's past experiences and how to decontextualize them — that is, remove the ideas from their context, generalize them, and make them abstract. The issue then for the writer is not "Should context clues be used?" but rather, "What is the best way to put words into a meaningful context?"

Able writers use a variety of contextual phrases as they explain certain hard words in their manuscripts. Here are some different kinds of context clues used in articles in the *World Book Encyclopedia* (Nault, 1978).[2]

Formal definition

A seismograph is an instrument for recording the direction, intensity, and duration of earthquakes.

Tennis is a game in which opposing players — one or two on each side — use rackets to hit a ball back and forth over a net.

Example

In hundreds of thousands of years, erosion can wear away a mountain until it is level with the plain.

If we used rebus writing in English, we could draw a sign for the word "bee" followed by a sign for the word "leaf" to stand for the word "belief."

Description

The eyes of the river hippopotamus stick out of his head. The position of the ears, eyes, and nostrils enables the animal to hear, see, and breathe with most of its head underwater.

The internal-combustion engine produces power by burning fuel inside a closed cylinder. The hot gases from the burned mixture drive a piston or a rotor that turns a crankshaft.

Sentences

When writing abstract, difficult material, keep sentences as short as possible. It is true that you cannot make materials more understandable just by shortening the sentences, but the length of a sentence influences its difficulty. In long sentences, for example, conjunctions such as *either-or, however, consequently, although, nevertheless, otherwise,* and *whereas* signal qualifying clauses.

The burden on short-term memory is greater for long sentences. The reader must remember what has just been said and then read on to see what qualifications

---

[2]For twenty-five years Edgar Dale was a readability consultant for *World Book Encyclopedia*.

have been made. Therefore, a long sentence is usually more difficult to remember. Somewhere between the first word and the last word, readers may lose the gist of your meaning. Their memory spans may not be great enough to remember the whole sentence.

Some scholars fear that their writing may be thought of as "oversimplified." Theodore Levitt of the Harvard School of Business has noted this problem in the world of academia:

> ...If something reads easily, and makes obvious good sense, then obviously it's only pap. No substance. If it reads as if translated from the German, that's substance. If it's written in the universal foreign language of integral calculus, that's high quality substance. The bigger the theory the better. (Levitt, 1978)

Philosopher and mathematician Bertrand Russell pointed out that one becomes acceptable as a writer of simple materials once he has passed the test of writing successfully for his colleagues (1958).

In summary, your writing should be neither harder nor easier than necessary. At times it should be hard enough to challenge the readers, but it should not be so hard that it frustrates. Ask yourself:

1. Have I removed technical terms not necessary for instructing the readers? When technical and difficult words are necessary, have I included concise and understandable definitions?
2. Do I have a glossary of the hard, important words that are unfamiliar to my readers?
3. Have I used varied contextual explanations for difficult vocabulary and ideas? Do I have enough concrete explanatory materials? Do I have unnecessary explanatory material?
4. Can any of my sentences be shortened, particularly sentences which contain complex or abstract information?

Organization and Appeal

Effective writing is well organized and provides thoughtful summaries. The able writer knows that the reader's attention must be captured immediately. Lengthy introductory remarks should be avoided. Polish up your opening paragraphs, because if page one is dull, your audience may never discover the important information you offer later.

Journalists know the value of an inviting lead sentence. Successful newsmen make it their business to write vivid, colorful leads.

> "In most of South America, political power is conferred by the barracks rather than the ballot box." (*Time*, July 31, 1978, p. 36)

Your material not only requires an interesting beginning but also must be well mapped and organized throughout. Your ideas need to be presented in logical, step-by-step order so that the reader can follow your line of thought. Each important idea should be clearly developed and explained.

As you organize your material, remember that even though *you* know your subject thoroughly, your *reader* may have little or no understanding of it. To you, what may seem simple, even elementary, may be complicated and confusing to a reader. One of the chief errors in communication is to assume that what is known by the writer is also known to the audience.

People who give directions (and much writing is the giving of directions) do not always understand the complexity of what they are communicating. Ask someone in a strange city how to get to a post office or other prominent building, and you will often be given directions that would be clear only to a person who already knows how to get there. About half the time the directions given will include, "you can't miss it." But you do. This error is known as the COIK fallacy. The term COIK stands for *Clear Only If Known*.

Sometimes both our written and spoken explanations are overly complex and introduce unnecessary and distracting elements. We include too much detail or else we leave out an important piece of information.

One way to avoid this problem is to emphasize *key points*. Key points are pivotal points. These are the ideas to watch out for when you are teaching a complicated skill. They are points where errors may occur. Key points are often the ideas that prove to be stumbling blocks for readers or learners.

The key point in striking a match, for example, is to strike it away from you. This is not hard to do, but it is important for safety's sake. Here are some key points for sautéing presented by Julia Child (1961, p. 13). Not a word is wasted.

1. The sautéing fat must be very hot, almost smoking, before food goes into the pan, otherwise there will be no sealing-in of juices, and no browning...
2. The food must be absolutely dry. If it is damp, a layer of steam develops between the food and the fat preventing the browning and searing process.
3. The pan must not be crowded. Enough air space must be left between each piece of food or it will steam rather than brown, and its juices will escape and burn in the pan.

One way to determine key points in your article or chapter is to ask yourself: What questions are essential to answer? Use concrete examples as you develop your answers, your key points.

Several years ago, questions were used by the state of Ohio as one source of curriculum data for preparing a new course of study in health. High school students were asked to write questions that they wanted answered. More than 2,700 questions were reported from the sixteen cooperating schools, many of which would not have been thought important by the course developers. Here are some of the questions asked:

1. What are some good home exercises for developing the body?
2. What are the best games for crippled children?
3. Why am I winded when I run a short distance?
4. How much sweet food should a person eat?
5. Should every city have a sewage-disposal plant?
6. Is it harmful to study after eating?
7. How can one become less self-conscious when one recites?
8. Is it harmful to marry a relative?
9. How do humans reproduce?
10. Why don't we have hoofs like a horse?

Well-organized material provides occasional repetition and a thoughtful summary. Readers want to remember what they have read, but sometimes even good readers get lost. They need an occasional assist from the writer to jog their memory and get them back on the right track.

The skillful writer helps the readers see the relationships between various parts of the article, that is, its structure. A backward glance now and then by the writer helps tell the readers where they have been. These reminders should not be just reruns of earlier ideas but fresh ways of presenting the material. Mere repetition is not good enough.

A summary doesn't just "play it again," but adds new insights while it weaves together various strands of information. It often provides the "so what" to your material. It explains what you have been driving at. A thoughtful summary can be the capstone (a finishing touch) of your article. To check the organization of your material you might ask:

1. Do my opening paragraphs catch the reader's interest?
2. Are my ideas arranged logically? Can the reader proceed step by step?
3. Have I discovered and covered all the key points in my material?
4. If I am trying to teach my reader to perform a particular task, have I given adequate, clear directions?
5. Do I provide a review of my information throughout the article?
6. Did I summarize my main points in a new way or was my summary a rehash?

The next step in writing effectively is to *edit your copy*. Review each section to see if it suits your audience and the nature of your material, and whether it is written in a clear, simple, well-organized manner. Eliminate, add, change, until your revision represents your best efforts in thinking and writing. Try the material out on readers in your targeted audience. Then and only then is your job finished.

APPENDIX A

Summary of Research on Optimal Sample Size

1958	Zimmerman	3 world history junior and senior high school textbooks, 600 to 800 pages. One sample every 40th or 50th page reported the same readability score as one sample every 10th page.
1962	Miller	6 middle grade non-fiction books of about 180 pages. Readability scores essentially the same for one sample every 10th, 20th, 30th, 40th, and 50th page.
1971	Martin & Lee	5 high school biology textbooks. No significant difference between sample schemes ranging from approximately one sample each for every 10 pages and one sample every 50 pages.
1975	Chall	66 articles from a popular children's encyclopedia resulted in similar scores for 33 articles, for 22 articles, for 13, and for 6 articles.
1976	Burkhead & Ulferts	48 college level management texts ranging in length from 120 to 720 pages. Samples taken at 20-, 30-, 40- and 50-page intervals were as reliable as those taken at 10-page intervals.
1983	Harris-Sharples	14 social studies and science textbooks ranging from 84 to 813 pages. Samples every 100th, 50th, 40th, 30th and 20th page. A minimum of 8 samples produced readability scores similar to the largest samples.

Appendix B

Examples of Text from Widely Known Books, Newspapers and Magazines

To clarify the scoring and to give the user a sense of what the various readability scores mean, we present excerpts from widely read books, newspapers, and magazines. They illustrate the readability levels — from grade 1 to college graduate levels — and help the user gain a "feel" for the various readability levels.

All but the first excerpt have 100 words, and report the unfamiliar words (underlined), the number of sentences and the cloze and reading level scores.

Reading Level 1

One morning Toad sat in bed.

"I have many things to do," he said.

"I will write them all down on a list so that I can remember them."

Toad wrote on a piece of paper: A list of things to do today.

Then he wrote:

Wake up.

"I have done that," said Toad, and he crossed it out:

From: *Frog and Toad Together*

Readability Data

Number of Words in Sample	60
Number of Whole Sentences	6
Number of Unfamiliar Words	0
Number of Sentences Per 100 Words*	10
Number of Unfamiliar Words Per 100 Words*	0
Cloze Score	57
Reading Level	1

*For samples shorter than 100 words, see Chapter 2, pages 7-8.)

Reading Level 2

"You said you didn't want it," said Thelma. "And anyhow, I don't want to sell it now."

"Why not?" said Frances.

"Well," said Thelma, "it is a very good tea set. It is plastic that does not break.

It has pretty red flowers on it.

It has all the cups and saucers.

It has the sugar bowl and the cream pitcher and the teapot.

It is almost new, and I think it cost a lot of money."

"I have two dollars and seventeen cents," said Frances.

"That's a lot of money."

"I don't know," said Thelma.

"If I sell you ...."

Readability Data

Number of Words in Sample	100
Number of Whole Sentences........	12
Number of Unfamiliar Words	3
Cloze Score	55
Reading Level	2

From: *A Bargain for Frances*

Reading Level 3

Once upon a time a very small witch was walking in the woods. The cold wind was blowing the dry leaves all around her. The little witch was frantically searching for a house for the winter. She could not find one. Suddenly a piece of orange paper, blown by the wind, landed at her feet. She picked it up.

The little witch looked closely at the paper and then she said, "I shall make myself a little house from this piece of orange paper."

She folded the paper in half. Then she took her scissors (she always carried a pair ....

Readability Data

Number of Words in Sample	100
Number of Whole Sentences........	8
Number of Unfamiliar Words	3
Cloze Score	53
Reading Level	3

From: *Highlights for Children*

Reading Level 4

Seals are wonderful <u>divers</u>. Some seals can dive several hundred feet below the surface. On deep dives, they can stay underwater up to 40 minutes without surfacing to breathe. They have special <u>features</u> to help save <u>oxygen</u> on such dives. When seals dive, they stop breathing. For very deep dives, their blood flows to everything except <u>critical</u> organs stops or slows. Seals can also slow their heart rates, sometimes to one-tenth the rates at the surface.

You may wonder how seals <u>avoid</u> the *bends* on deep dives. The bends are a painful <u>condition</u>. They are caused when <u>nitrogen</u> <u>dissolves</u> in ....

From: *The Harp Seal*

Readability Data

Number of Words in Sample 100
Number of Whole Sentences 9
Number of Unfamiliar Words 8
Cloze Score 49
Reading Level 4

Reading Level 5-6

Eskimos of <u>Alaska's</u> <u>Arctic</u> north coast have hunted whales for <u>centuries</u>.

<u>Survival</u> has depended on killing the 60-foot-long bowhead whales that swim from the <u>Bering</u> Sea to the ice-<u>clogged</u> <u>Beaufort</u> Sea each Spring. The Eskimos' <u>entire</u> way of life has been centered around the hunt.

But now that way of life is being <u>threatened</u> by America's need for oil, say many Eskimos who hunt the whales.

Huge amounts of oil may be beneath the Beaufort Sea. And oil companies want to begin drilling this spring.

However, many Eskimos say <u>severe</u> storms and ice <u>conditions</u> make drilling dangerous ....

From: *My Weekly Reader*, Edition 6

Readability Data

Number of Words in Sample 100
Number of Whole Sentences 6
Number of Unfamiliar Words 11
Cloze Score 42
Reading Level 5-6

Reading Level 7-8

Why is it that as soon as "Jingle Bells" starts playing on the radio, otherwise-sane people are driven to extremes to create the Perfect Christmas? Take the case of Maureen McFadden, a *Woman's Day* editor, who decided to decorate her tree with homemade gingerbread ornaments. "I started late in the evening," she recalled. "And then I knocked the molasses jar on the floor." It was downhill from there. Her cat—long-haired, of course—sat in the molasses pool. "And when I yelped, he ran down the hall into my bedroom spewing molasses everywhere." Still, after she washed the ....

From: *Woman's Day*

Readability Data

Number of Words in Sample	100
Number of Whole Sentences	7
Number of Unfamiliar Words	19
Cloze Score	36
Reading Level	7-8

Reading Level 9-10

The controversy over the laser-armed satellite boils down to two related questions: Will it be technically effective? And should the United States make a massive effort to deploy it?

To its backers, the laser seems the perfect weapon. Traveling in a straight line at 186,000 miles per second, a laser beam is tens of thousands of times as fast as any bullet or rocket. It could strike its target with a power of many watts per square inch. The resulting heat, combined with a mechanical shock wave created by recoil as surface layers were blasted away, would quickly melt ....

From: *Discover*

Readability Data

Number of Words in Sample	100
Number of Whole Sentences	5
Number of Unfamiliar Words	23
Cloze Score	28
Reading Level	9-10

Reading Level 11-12

The latest finding is a <u>refinement</u> of <u>evidence</u> presented last summer by <u>audio</u> <u>expert</u> <u>James</u> <u>Barger</u> — who <u>testified</u> there was a 50 <u>percent</u> <u>probability</u> that four shots were recorded on the tape. Barger had recorded test <u>firings</u> at <u>various</u> points in the <u>Dealey</u> <u>Plaza</u>, then <u>compared</u> them with the motorcycle recording. The greatest <u>similarity</u> was <u>produced</u> by two shots from the book <u>depository</u>, one from the <u>knoll</u> and another from the <u>depository</u>. But Barger did not draw <u>firm</u> <u>conclusions</u> because he could not pinpoint the policeman's motorcycle; his <u>estimate</u> could have been 18 feet off in any direction. <u>Weiss</u>, whose ....

From: *Newsweek*

Readability Data
Number of Words in Sample 100
Number of Whole Sentences 4
Number of Unfamiliar Words 23
Cloze Score 25
Reading Level 11-12

Reading Level 13-15

Until the <u>1940's</u>, there were no <u>specific</u> <u>psychiatric</u> drugs. <u>Bromides</u>, <u>barbiturates</u>, and <u>opiates</u> were known to <u>sedate</u> <u>disturbed</u> <u>patients</u> but did not <u>reverse</u> the <u>symptoms</u> of <u>severe</u> <u>mental</u> <u>illnesses</u> such as the <u>schizophrenias</u> or <u>manic-depressive</u> <u>psychoses</u>. They did <u>ameliorate</u> <u>anxiety</u>, but only at the cost of fogging the minds of the <u>recipients</u>, who had to decide between being unhappy and being <u>intoxicated</u>. In the <u>1950's</u>, the first <u>specific</u> drug appeared: <u>chlorpromazine</u> (trade name <u>Thorazine</u>). It was <u>synthesized</u> when an <u>antihistamine</u> <u>chemical</u> <u>relative</u> was found to <u>sedate</u> <u>surgical</u> <u>patients</u>. However, <u>clinical</u> <u>observations</u> showed that this drug did much more than simply ....

From: *Psychology Today*

Readability Data
Number of Words in Sample 100
Number of Whole Sentences 5
Number of Unfamiliar Words 35
Cloze Score 17
Reading Level 13-15

Reading Level 16+

Further <u>support</u> for the view that <u>edu-cational</u> <u>expansion</u> would <u>reduce</u> <u>inequali-ties</u> was <u>derived</u> from the <u>dualistic</u> nature of <u>developing</u> <u>societies</u>. The <u>economic</u> <u>structures</u> of <u>developing</u> <u>societies</u> were said to <u>consist</u> of two <u>sectors</u>: a <u>traditional</u> <u>sector</u> that uses little capital, is <u>relatively</u> <u>unproductive</u>, does not <u>require</u> an <u>edu-cated</u> <u>labor</u> force, and places a great <u>emphasis</u> on <u>subsistence</u> farming, small workshops and small commercial <u>enter-prises</u>; and a modern <u>sector</u> that uses <u>advanced</u> <u>technology</u> and capital, is far more <u>productive</u>, and <u>requires</u> a <u>labor</u> force with at least some schooling. <u>Ex-panding</u> the <u>educational</u> <u>system</u> would <u>qualify</u> more <u>workers</u> for jobs where <u>de-mands</u> ....

From: *Harvard Educational Review*

Readability Data

Number of Words in Sample 100
Number of Whole Sentences 2
Number of Unfamiliar Words 37
Cloze Score .... -6
Reading Level .... 16+

BIBLIOGRAPHY

Anderson, R. C., & Freebody, P. (1981). Vocabulary knowledge. In J. T. Guthrie (Ed.), *Comprehension and Teaching* (pp. 77-117). Newark, DE: International Reading Association.

Agnihotri, R. K., & Khanna, A. L. (1992). Evaluating the readability of school textbooks: An Indian study. *Journal of Reading, 35*:4, 282-288.

Armbruster, B. B. (1984). The problem of inconsiderate text. In G. Duffey (Ed.), *Comprehension Instruction* (pp. 202-217). New York: Longman.

Bamberger, R., & Rabin, A. T. (1984). New approach to readability. *The Reading Teacher, 37*, 512-519.

Barnhart, C. L. (Ed.) (1952). *Thorndike-Barnhart high school dictionary.* Chicago: Scott, Foresman.

Barzun, J. (1975). *Simple and direct: A rhetoric for writers.* New York: Harper & Row.

Becker, W. (1978). Teaching reading and language to the disadvantaged. *Harvard Educational Review, 47*, pp. 518-543.

Bell, J. H., & Johnson, R. E. (1992) *Effect of lowering the reading level of a health education pamphlet on increasing comprehension by ESL adults.* Grant study for Research and Development Committee, Calgary General Hospital, Alberta, Canada.

Bjornsson, C. H. (1983). Readability of newspapers in 11 languages. *Reading Research Quarterly, 18*, 480-497.

Bormuth, J. R. (1964). Readability: A new approach. *Reading Research Quarterly, 1*, 79-132.

Bormuth, J. R. (1967). Comparable cloze and multiple-choice comprehension test scores. *Journal of Reading, 10*, 291-299.

Bormuth, J. R. (1968). Cloze test readability: Criterion scores. *Journal of Educational Measurement, 5*, 189-196.

Bormuth, J. R. (1969, March). *Development of readability analyses* (Final Report, Project No. 7- 0052, Contract No. 1, OEC-3-7-070052-0326). Washington, DC: Department of Health, Education and Welfare. (ERIC Document Reproduction Service No. ED 054 233).

Bormuth, J. R. (1971). *Development of standards of readability: Report of development* (Project No. 9-0237). Chicago: University of Chicago. (ERIC Document Reproduction Service No. ED 054-233).

Botta, R. (1993). Does shorter mean easier to understand? A study of comprehension of *USA Today* information stories. Paper presented at the Annual Meeting of the Association for Education and Journalism and Mass Communication (76th, Kansas City, MO, August 1993).

Buckingham, B. R., & Dolch, E. W. (1936). *A combined word list.* Boston: Ginn.

Calfee, R. C., & Curley, R. (1984). Structures of prose in the content areas. In J. Flood (Ed.), *Understanding reading comprehension* (pp. 161-180). Newark, DE: International Reading Association.

Carroll, J. B., Davies, P., & Richman, B. (1971). *Word frequency book.* New York: Macmillan.

Carroll, J. B. (1987). The National Assessments in Reading: Are we misreading the findings? *Phi Delta Kappan,* 414-430.

Carver, R. P. (1975-76). Measuring prose difficulty using the reading scale. *Reading Research Quarterly, 11*:4, 660-685.

Carver, R. P. (1985). Measuring readability using DRP units. *Journal of Reading Behavior, 17*, 303-316.

Carver, R. P. (1990). Predicting accuracy of comprehension from the relative difficulty of the material. *Learning and Individual Differences, 2*, 405-422.

Caylor, J. S., Sticht, T. G., Fox, L. C., & Ford, J. P. (1973, March). *Methodologies for determining reading requirements of military occupational specialties* (Technical Report No. 73-75). HumRRO Western Division. Presidio of Monterey, CA: Human Resources Research Organization.

Chall, J. S. (1956). A survey of users of the Dale-Chall formula. *Educational Research Bulletin, 35*, 197-212.

Chall, J. S. (1958; reprinted, 1974). *Readability: An appraisal of research and application.* Bureau of Educational Research Monographs, No. 34. Columbus, OH: Ohio State University Press. Reprinted (1974) by Bowker Publishing Co., Ltd., Epping, Essex, England.

Chall, J. S. (1975). An analysis of the readability of articles of *The New Book of Knowledge.* Unpublished research report.

Chall, J. S. (1979, October 29). Readability: In search of improvement. *Publishers Weekly, 216*:18, 40-41.

Chall, J. S. (1981, August). Readability: Conceptions and misconceptions. *SLATE Newsletter.* Urbana, IL: National Council of Teachers of English.

Chall, J. S. (1983a). *Learning to read: The great debate,* Updated edition. New York: McGraw-Hill. (3rd edition, in press, 1995.)

Chall, J. S. (1983b). *Stages of reading development.* New York: McGraw-Hill. (2nd edition, in press, 1995.)

Chall, J. S. (1984). Readability and prose comprehension: Continuities and discontinuities. In J. Flood (Ed.), *Understanding Reading Comprehension.* Newark, DE: International Reading Association.

Chall, J. S. (1988). The beginning years. In B. L. Zakaluk & S. J. Samuels (Eds.), *Readability: Its past, present and future* (pp. 2-13). Newark, DE: International Reading Association.

Chall, J. S., Bissex, G., Conard, S. S., & Harris-Sharples, S. (in press). *Holistic assessment of texts: Scales for estimating the difficulty of literature, social studies, and science materials.*

Chall, J. S., & Conard, S. S. (1991). *Should textbooks challenge students? The case for easier or harder books.* New York: Teachers College Press.

Chall, J. S., Conard, S. S., & Harris, S. (1977). *An analysis of textbooks in relation to declining SAT scores.* Princeton, NJ: Educational Testing Service and the College Entrance Examination Board.

Chall, J. S., & Dale, E. (1950). Familiarity of selected health terms. *Educational Research Bulletin, 29,* 197-206.

Chall, J. S., Freeman, A., & Levy, B. (1982). Minimum competency testing of reading: An analysis of eight tests designed for grade 11. In G. Mandaus (Ed.), *The courts, validity, and minimum competency testing.* Boston: Kluwer-Nijhoff Publishing.

Chall, J. S., Jacobs, V. A., & Baldwin, L. E. (1990). *The reading crisis: Why poor children fall behind.* Cambridge, MA: Harvard University Press.

Child, J. (1961). *Mastering the art of French cooking* (Vol. 1). New York: Alfred A. Knopf.

Clay, M. M. (1991). *Becoming literate: The construction of inner control.* Portsmouth, NH: Heinemann.

Cole, L. (1940). *The teacher's handbook of technical vocabulary.* Bloomington, IL: Public School Publishing Co.

College Entrance Examination Board (1980 and later editions). *Degrees of reading power (DRP).* Princeton, NJ: College Entrance Examination Board.

Cullinan, B., & Fitzgerald, S. (1984). *Background information bulletin on the use of readability formulas.* Urbana, IL: National Council of Teachers of English.

Dale, E. (1929). *Factual basis for curriculum revision in arithmetic with special reference to children's understanding of business terms.* Unpublished doctoral dissertation, University of Chicago, Chicago, IL.

Dale, E. (1931a). Evaluating Thorndike's word list. *Educational Research Bulletin, 10,* 451-457.

Dale, E. (1931b). A comparison of two word lists. *Educational Research Bulletin, 10,* 484-489.

Dale, E., & Chall, J. S. (1948). *A formula for predicting readability.* Columbus, OH: Ohio State University Bureau of Educational Research. (Reprinted from *Educational Research Bulletin, 27,* 11-20, 37-54)

Dale, E., & Chall, J. S. (1949). The concept of readability. *Elementary English, 26,* 19-26.

Dale, E., & Eichholz, G. (1960). *Children's knowledge of words: An interim report.* Columbus, OH: The Ohio State University.

Dale, E., & Hager, H. (1950). *Some suggestions for writing health materials.* New York: National Tuberculosis Association.

Dale, E., & O'Rourke, J. (1971). *Techniques of teaching vocabulary.* Menlo Park, CA: Benjamin/Cummings Publishing Co.

Dale, E., & O'Rourke, J. (1976). *The living word vocabulary: The words we know.* Elgin, IL: Field Enterprises Educational Corp.

Dale, E., & O'Rourke, J. (1981). *The living word vocabulary.* Chicago: World Book/Childcraft International.

Dale, E., & Razik, T. (Supervisors of compilation). (1963). *Bibliography of vocabulary studies* (2nd rev. ed.). Columbus, OH: Ohio State University Bureau of Educational Research. (See also 1973 edition).

Davis, F. (1972). Psychometric research on comprehension in reading. *Reading Research Quarterly, 7,* 628-678.

Davison, A., & Kantor, R. N. (1982). On the failure of readability formulas to define readable texts: A case study from adoptions. *Reading Research Quarterly, 17,* 187-209.

Deford, D. E., Lyons, C. A., & Pinnel, G. S. (Eds.). (1991). *Bridges to literacy: Learning from reading recovery.* Portsmouth, NH: Heinemann.

Dolch, E. W. (1939). Fact burden and reading difficulty. *Elementary English Review, 16,* 135-138.

Dolch, E. W. (1948a). The first thousand words for children's reading. In *Problems in reading* (pp. 108-129). Champaign, IL: Garrard Press.

Dolch, E. W. (1948b). *Problems in reading.* Champaign, IL: Garrard Press.

Feifel, H., & Lorge, I. (1950). Qualitative differences in the vocabulary responses of children. *Journal of Educational Psychology, 41,* 1-18.

FitzGerald, F. (1979) *America revised.* New York: Vintage Books.

Flesch, R. (1943). *Marks of readable style: A study in adult education.* New York: Bureau of Publications, Teachers College, Columbia Univerisy.

Flesch, R. (1948). A new readability yardstick. *Journal of Applied Psychology, 32,* 221-233.

Flesch, R. (1951). *The Associated Press writing handbook.* New York: Associated Press.

Flesch, R. (1949 & 1974). *The art of readable writing: With the Flesch readability formula.* New York: Harper & Row.

Frase, L. T. (1980, April). *Computer aids for writing and text design.* Symposium presented at the annual meeting of the American Educational Research Association, Boston.

Freebody, P., & Anderson, R. C. (1983). Effects of vocabulary difficulty, text cohesion, and schema availability on reading comprehension. *Reading Research Quarterly, 18,* 277-294.

Fry, E. (1968). A readability formula that saves time. *Journal of Reading, 11,* 513-516, 575- 578.

Fry, E. B. (1977). Fry's Readability Graph: Clarifications, validity, and extension to level 17. *Journal of Reading 21,* 242-252. (Hand calculator for the Fry readability scale (extended) available from Jamestown Publishers, P.O. Box 6713, Providence, RI 02940.)

Fry, E. (1989). Reading Formulas: Maligned but valid. *Journal of Reading, 32,* 292-297.

Gates, A. I. (1926). *A reading vocabulary for the pri-

mary grades. New York: Teachers College, Columbia University.

Gates, A. I. (1930). *Interest and ability in reading.* New York: Macmillan.

Gates, A. I. (1935). *A reading vocabulary for the primary grades* (revised). New York:Teachers College, Columbia University.

Gates, A. I. (1937). *Spelling difficulties in 3,876 words.* New York: Teachers College, Columbia University.

The Gates-MacGinitie Reading Tests (Third Edition, 1989). Chicago, IL: The Riverside Publishing Company.

Goltz, C. R. (1964). Computation of readability scores. *Journal of Developmental Reading. 7,* 175-187.

Goodman, K., & Bird, L. B. (1984). On the wording of texts: A study of the intra-text word frequency. *Research in the Teaching of English, 18*:2, 119-145.

Gray, W. S., & Leary, B. E. (1935). *What makes a book readable.* Chicago: University of Chicago Press.

Greene, H. A. (1954). *The new Iowa spelling scale.* Iowa City, IA: University of Iowa.

Grove, P. B. (Editor-in-chief) (1961). *Webster's third new international dictionary of the English language* (unabridged). Springfield, MA: G. & C. Merriam Company.

Gunning, R. (1952, 1968). *The technique of clear writing.* New York: McGraw-Hill.

Harris, A. J. and Jacobson, M. D. (1972 & 1982). *Basic elementary reading vocabularies.* New York: Macmillan.

Harris-Sharples, S. (1982, December). *Readability analysis of information on Diazide patient sheets.* Philadelphia, PA: Smith, Kline and French.

Harris-Sharples, S. (1983a). *Study of the "match" between student reading ability and textbook difficulty during classroom instruction.* Unpublished doctoral dissertation. Cambridge, MA: Harvard Graduate School of Education.

Harris-Sharples, S. (1983b). *An analysis of social studies and science textbooks.* Unpublished research report.

Hayes, D., Wolfer, L., & Wolfe, M. (1993). *Was the decline in SAT scores caused by simplified school texts?* Paper presented at the Annual Meeting of the American Sociological Association, Miami, FL.

Hillerich, R. L. (1978). *A writing vocabulary of elementary children.* Springfield, IL: Charles C. Thomas.

Horn, E. (1937). *Methods of instruction in the social studies.* New York: Charles Scribners Sons.

Horn, M. (1928). *A study of the vocabulary of children before entering first grade.* Washington, DC: Child Study Committee of the International Kindergarten Union, Association for Childhood Education.

Hunt, K. (1965). *Grammatical structures written at three grade levels.* National council of Teachers of English Report No. 3. Urbana, IL: National Council of Teachers of English.

Irwin, J. W. (1988). Linguistic cohesion and the developing reader/writer. *Topics in Language Disorders, 8*:3, 14-23.

Johnson, D. D., Moe, A. J., & Baumann, J. F. (1983). *The Ginn word book for teachers: A basic lexicon.* Lexington, MA: Ginn and Company.

Jones, K. H. (1993). *Analysis of readability and interest in home economics textbooks for special needs learners.* Paper presented at the American Vocational Association Convention. (Nashville, TN, December 1993).

Kemper, S. (1983). Measuring the inference load of a text. *Journal of Educational Psychology, 75*:3, 391-401.

Kemper, S. (1993). Enhancing older adults' reading comprehension. *Discourse Processes, 16*:4, 405-428.

Kemper, S., Jackson, J. D., Cheung, H., & Anagnopoulos, C. A. (in press, *Discourse Processes*). Enhancing older adults' reading comprehension.

Kilty, T. (1979). *Familiarity of mathematical terms.* Unpublished manuscript.

Kincaid, J. P., Aagard, J. A., & O'Hara, J. W. (1980). *Development and test of a computer readability editing system (CRES)* (TAEG Report No. 83). U.S. Navy Training Analysis and Evaluation Group, Orlando, FL.

Kincaid, J. P., Aagard, J. A., O'Hara, J. W., & Cottrell, L. K. (1981, March). Computer readability editing system. *TEEE Transactions on Professional Communications.*

Kintsch, W. (1979). On modeling comprehension. *Educational Psychologist, 14,* 3-14.

Kintsch, W. (1994). Text comprehension, memory, and learning. *American Psychologist, 49*:4, 294-303.

Kintsch, W., Britton, B. K., Fletcher, C. R., Kintsch, E., Mannes, S.M., & Mitchell, J.N. (in press). *A comprehension-based approach to learning and understanding.*

Kintsch, W., & Miller, J. R. (1981). Readability: A view from cognitive psychology. In *Teaching: Research Reviews.* Neward, DE: International Reading Association.

Kintsch, W., & Vipond, D. (1977, June). Reading comprehension and readability in educational practice. Paper presented at the Conference on Memory, University of Uppsala. (see the published version, 1979).

Kintsch, W., & Vipond, E. (1979). Reading comprehension and readability in educational practice and psychological theory. In L.G. Nilsson (Ed.), *Perspectives on Memory Research.* Hillsdale, NJ: Erlbaum.

Klare, G. R. (1952). A table for rapid determination of Dale-Chall readability scores. *Educational Research Bulletin, 31,* 43-47.

Klare, G. R. (1963). *The measurement of readability.* Ames, IA: Iowa State University Press.

Klare, G. R. (1974-75). Assessing readability. *Reading Research Quarterly, 10,* 62-102.

Klare, G. R. (1984). Readability. In P. D. Pearson (Ed.), *Handbook of reading research* (pp. 681-744).

New York: Longman.

Klare, G. R. (1988). The formative years. In B. L. Zakaluk & S.J. Samuels (Eds.), *Readability: Its past, present, and future* (pp. 14-34). Newark, DE: International Reading Association.

Kucera, H., & Francis, W. N. (1967). *Computational analysis of present-day AmericanEnglish*. Providence, RI: Brown University Press.

Levitt, T. (1978). From *Innovator, 10*:6. (The University of Michigan School of Education Report to the President of the University, Robben W. Fleming, for the year 1977-78, by Wilbur J. Cohen, Dean, School of Education.)

Lorge, I. (1939). Predicting reading difficulty of selections for children. *Elementary English Review, 16*, 229-233.

Lorge, I. (1944). Predicting readability. *Teachers College Record, 45*, 404-419.

Lorge, I. (1949). *The semantic count of the 570 commonest English words*. New York: Bureau of Publications, Teachers College, Columbia University.

Lorge, I., & Chall, J. S. (1963). Estimating the size of vocabularies of children and adults: An analysis of methodological issues. *The Journal of Experimental Education, 32*, 147-157.

Lyons, L. M. (1965). *Reporting the news*. Cambridge, MA: Harvard University Press.

MacDonald, N. H., Frase, L. T., Gingrich, P. S., & Keenan, S. A. (1982). The writer's workbench: computer aids for text analysis. *Educational Psychologist, 17*, 172-179.

MacGinitie, W., & Tretiak, R. (1971). Sentence depth measures as predictors of reading difficulty. *Reading Research Quarterly, 6*, 364-376.

Maeroff, G. I. (1975, October 11). *The New York Times*, p. 1.

Martin, M., & Lee, W. (1971). Sample frequency of application of Dale-Chall readability formula. *Educational Research Bulletin, 40*, 145-148.

McCall, W. A., & Crabbs, L. M. (1926, revised 1979). *Standard test lessons in reading*. New York: Teachers College, Columbia University Press.

McKeown, M. G., & Curtis, M. E. (Eds.). (1987). *The nature of vocabulary acquisition*. Hillsdale, NJ: Erlbaum.

Meyer, B. J. F. (1982, February). Reading research and the composition teacher: The importance of plans. *College Composition and Communication, 33*:1, 37-49.

Meyer, B. J. F. (in press) Text processing of everyday task performance.

Miller, G. R., & Coleman, E. B. (1967). A set of thirty-six prose passages calibrated for complexity. *Journal of Verbal Learning and Verbal Behavior, 6*, 851-854.

Miller, H. (1962). *Comparison of six trade books*. Unpublished seminar paper, City College of New York.

Miller, J. R., & Kintsch, W. (1980). Readability and recall of short prose passages: A theoretical analysis. *Journal of Experimental Psychology: Human Learning and Memory, 6*, 335-354.

Moe, A. J., Hopkins, C. J., & Rush, R. T. (1982). *The vocabulary of first-grade children*. Springfield, IL: Charles C. Thomas.

Morriss, E. C., & Holversen, D. (1938). *Idea analysis technique*. Unpublished paper, Teachers College, Columbia University, New York, NY. In Chall, J.S. (1958). *Readability: An appraisal of research and application*. Columbus, OH: Ohio State University Press.

Nagy, W. E. (1986). *The influence of word and text properties on learning from context*. Cambridge, MA: Bolt, Beranek & Newman, Inc.

National Assessment of Educational Progress (NAEP) (1985). *The Reading Report Card*. Princeton, NJ: Educational Testing Service.

Nault, W. H. (Ed.). (1978 and 1984). *World book encyclopedia*. Chicago: World Book/Childcraft International, Inc.

Norman, S., Kemper, S., & Kynette, D. (1992). Adults' reading comprehension: Effects of syntactic complexity and working memory. *Journal of Gerontology: Psychological Sciences, 74*:4, 256-265.

Ogden, C. K. (1952). *Basic English* (Psyche Miniatures, General Series, No. 48). London: Basic English Publishing Co.

Ogden, C. K. (1954). *The basic words*. Psyche Miniatures, General Series No. 44. London: Kegan Paul.

Ogden, C. K. (1940; twentieth impression, 1974). *The general basic English dictionary*. London: Evans Brothers Limited.

O'Hear, M. F., & Ashton, P. J. (1989). Main idea clues. *Forum for Reading, 21*:1, 58-66.

Ojemann, R. (1934). The reading ability of parents and factors associated with the reading difficulty of parent education materials. In G. D. Stoddard (Ed.) *Researchers in Parent Education, II.* 19. (University of Iowa Studies, Studies in Child Welfare, VIII). Iowa City, IA: University of Iowa.

Pearson, P. D. (1974-75). The effects of grammatical complexity on children's comprehension, recall, and conception of certain semantic relations. *Reading Research Quarterly, 10*, 155- 192.

Pearson, P. D., & Camperell, K. (1981). Comprehension of text structures. In J.T. Guthrie (Ed.), *Comprehension and Teaching: Research Reviews*. Newark, DE: International Reading Association.

Perfetti, C. A. (1985). *Reading ability*. New York: Oxford University Press.

Peterson, B. (1991). Selecting books for beginning readers. In D. E. DeFord, C. A. Lyons, & G. S. Pinnell (Eds.), *Bridges to literacy: Learning from reading recovery* (pp.119-138). Portsmouth, NH: Heinemann.

Porter, D., & Popp, H. M. (1975). *Measuring the readability of children's trade books*. Report to the Ford Foundation.

Rabin, A. T. (1988). Determining difficulty levels of text written in languages other than English. In B. L. Zaluk & S. J. Samuels (Eds.), *Readability: Its past, present and future* (pp. 46-76). Newark,

DE: International Reading Association.

Rinsland, H. D. (1945). *A basic vocabulary of elementary school children*. New York: Macmillan.

Roswell, F. G., & Chall, J. S. (1991). DARTTS (Diagnostic Assessments of Reading and Trial Teaching Strategies). Chicago, IL: The Riverside Publishing Company.

Rush, R. T. (1984). *Assessing readability: Formulas and alternatives*. Paper presented at the Annual Meeting of the Wyoming State Reading Council of the International Reading Association. Rawlins, WY, October 5-6, 1984. ERIC document ED251801.

Russell, B. (1958). Portraits from memory. In R. Egner (Ed.), *Bertrand Russell's Best*. London: Allen Unwin.

Shelby, A. N. (1992). Readability formulas: one more time. *Management Communication Quarterly, 5*:4, pp 485-495.

Singer, H. (1975). The SEER technique: A non-computational procedure for quickly estimating readability levels. *Journal of Reading Behavior, 3*, 255-267.

Spache, G. (1962; revised 1974). The revised Spache readability formula. In G. Spache, *Good reading for poor readers*. Champaign, IL: Garrard Publishing Company.

Standal, T. (1987). Computer-measured readability. *Computers-in-the-Schools, 4*:1, 123-132.

Steinley, G. L. (1987). A framework for evaluating textbooks. *Clearing House, 61*:3, 114-118.

Stenner, A. J., Horabin, I., Smith, D. R., & Smith, M. (1988a). Most comprehension tests do measure reading comprehension: A response to McLean and Goldstein. *Phi Delta Kappan*, June 1988, 765-767.

Stenner, A. J., Horabin, I., Smith, D. R., & Smith. M. (1988b). *The lexile framework*. Durham, NC: Metametrics.

Sticht, T. G., Beck, L. J., Hauke, R. N., Kleiman, G. M., & James, J. H. (1974). *Auding and reading*. Alexandria, VA: Human Resources Research Organization.

Sticht, T. G., Caylor, J. S., Fox, L. C., Hauke, R. N., James, J. H., Snyder, S. S., & Kern, R. P. (1973, December). *HumRRO's literacy research for the literacy training*. Alexandria, VA: Human Resources Research Organization.

Strunk, W., & White, E. B. (1979). *Elements of style*. Third Edition. New York: Macmillan.

Taylor, W. (1953). Cloze procedure: A new tool for measuring readability. *Journalism Quarterly, 33*, 42-46.

Terman, L. M., & Merrill, M. A. (1973). *Stanford-Binet intelligence scale* (Third Revision). Chicago, IL: Riverside Publishing Company.

Thorndike, E. L. (1921). *A teacher's word book of 10,000 words*. New York: Teachers College, Columbia University.

Thorndike, E. L. (1931). *A teacher's word book of 20,000 words*. New York: Teachers College, Columbia University.

Thorndike, E. L., & Lorge, I. (1944). *The teacher's word book of 30,000 words*. New York: Bureau of Publications, Teachers College, Columbia University.

Thorndike, R. L. (1973-74). Reading as reasoning. *Reading Research Quarterly, 9*, 135-147.

Time, (1978, July 31), p. 36.

Treece, N. L. (1991). *An investigation into the use of the cloze procedure to measure the reading comprehension ability of hearing-impaired students*. Unpublished doctoral dissertation, Harvard Graduate School of Education, Cambridge, MA.

Trollinger, Jr. W. V., & Kaestle, C. F. (1991). High-brow and middlebrow magazines in 1920. In Kaestle, C. F., Damon-Moore, H., Stedman, L. C., Tinsley, K., & Trollinger, Jr., W. V. *Literacy in the United States*, New Haven, CT: Yale University Press.

Vachon, M. K., & Haney, R. E. (1991). A procedure for determining the level of abstraction of science reading material. *Journal of Research and Science Teaching, 28*:4, 343-352.

Venezky, R. L. (1982). The origins of the present-day chasm between adult literacy needs and school literacy instruction. *Visible Language, 16*, 113-126.

Vogel, M., & Washburne, C. (1928). An objective method of determining grade placement of children's reading material. *Elementary School Journal, 28*, 373-381.

Vygotsky, L. (1978). *Mind in society*. (M. Cole, V. John-Steiner, S. Scribner, & E. Souberman, Eds., & Trans.) Cambridge, MA: Harvard University Press.

Washburne, C. W. (1942). *The right book for the right child* (3rd edition). New York: John Day Company.

Washburne, C. W., & Vogel, M. (1926). *Winnetka graded book list*. Chicago: American Library Association.

Wechsler, D. (1974). *Manual for the Wechsler intelligence scale for children -- Revised*. New York: The Psychological Corporation.

West, M., & Endicott, J.G. (Eds.) (1961; 5th edition, 1976). *The new method English dictionary*. New York: Longman.

White, M. D. (1990). The readability of children's reference materials. *Library Quarterly, 60*:4, 300-319.

Young, S. (1984). *A theory and simulation of macrostructure*. Doctoral dissertation, University of Colorado.

Zeller, D. (1941). *The relative importance of factors of interest in reading materials for junior high school pupils*. New York: Bureau of Publications, Teachers College, Columbia University.

Zimmerman, R. (1958). *Comparison of three world history books for junior high school*. Unpublished seminar paper, City College of New York.

Zipf, G. K. (1935). *The psycho-biology of language*. Boston: Houghton Mifflin.

INDEX

level of vocabulary knowledge, 138
organization of material, 141
reader interest, 134
sentences, length of, 140
summaries, use of, 143
reading comprehension, 82
vocabulary as most important factor, 82
reading deficits, causes, 103
Reading Vocabulary for the Primary Grades, 120, 123, 124
Right Book for the Right Child, The, 50
Ringland, H.D., 127
Russell, Bertrand, 141

S
Saturday Evening Post, 101
Scholastic Aptitude Test, use of for readability measurement, 51
SEER (Singer's Eyeball Estimate of Readability), 109
Semantic Count of the 570 Commonest English Words, 120, 126
sentence length, predictor of comprehension difficulty, 5
Shelby, A.N., 113
Singer, H., 109
Spache, G., 50, 79, 120, 121, 127
Spelling Difficulties in 3,876 Words, 124, 130
Standard Test Lessons in Reading, 56
Stanford-Binet, 117
Stenner, A.J., Horabin, I., Smith, D.R., & Smith, M., 3, 89, 90, 94, 96, 98
Sticht, T.G., Beck, L.J., Hauke, R.N., Kleiman, G.M., & James, J.H., 48
Sticht, T.G., Gaylor, J.S., Fox, L.C., Hauke, R.H., James, J.H., Snyder, S.S., & Kern, R.P., 51
Stone, C., 121
structure of text, 107, 108
expository, 109
relationship to content, 107
Strunk, W., & White, E.B., 134
Study of the Vocabulary of Children Before Entering First Grade, 125

T
Taylor, W., 48, 83, 94

Teacher's Handbook of Technical Vocabulary, 120, 122
Teacher's Word Book, 119, 127
Teacher's Word Book of 20, 000 Words, 128
Teacher's Word Book of 30, 000 Words, 128
Technique of Teaching Vocabulary, 123, 128
Terman, L.M., & Merrill, M.A., 82, 117
textbooks, influence of on SAT scores, 88
Thorndike, E.L., 127, 128
Thorndike, E.L., & Lorge, I., 119, 128
Thorndike, R.L., 79, 82, 117, 118
Treece, M.L., 83
Trollinger, W.V., Jr., & Koestle, C.F., 101, 111, 112
T-Unit, 82, 83

V
Vachon, M.K., & Haney, R.E., 113
Venezky, R.L., 51
vocabulary, 117
in Dale-Chall formula, 117
levels of analysis of, 118
role in readability, 117
word length as measure of difficulty of, 118
Vocabulary of First-Grade Children, 126
vocabulary lists, historical perspective, 119
frequency scores, use of, 120
Vogel, M., & Washburne, C.W., 87
Vygotsky, L., 46

W
Washburne, C.W., 50
Washburne, C.W., & Vogel, M., 87
Wechsler, D., 82, 117
West, M., & Endicott, J.G., 129, 130
Word Frequency Book, 122
word length & difficulty, relationship of, 5, 81
word lists, uses and limitations of, 128
World Book, 50
writing & editing, use of formula for, 49
caution in use of, 50
Writing Vocabulary for Elementary Children, 125

Z
Zeller, D., 80
Zipf, G.K., 5, 82

ABOUT THE AUTHORS

Jeanne S. Chall, Ph.D. is emeritus professor, Harvard University, Graduate School of Education. She founded and directed the Harvard Reading Laboratory for 25 years.

Dr. Chall has written numerous books and articles, including *Readability: An Appraisal of Research and Application*; *Learning to Read: The Great Debate* (third edition, 1995); *Stages of Reading Development* (second edition, 1995); and *Should Textbooks Challenge Students? The Case for Easier and Harder Books*, with Sue Conard.

She is a member of the National Academy of Education and the Reading Hall of Fame, and has served on the Board of Directors of the International Reading Association and the National Society for the Study of Education.

She has received many awards, including the American Psychological Association's Edward L. Thorndike Award for distinguished psychological contributions to education; the American Educational Research Association Award for Distinguished Research in Education; and the International Reading Association Citation of Merit.

Edgar Dale, Ph.D. was Professor of Education and research associate, Bureau of Educational Research, Ohio State University. From 1935 to 1971 he wrote and edited *The Newsletter*, which was distributed to 25,000 readers in the United States and internationally. His book *Can You Give the Public What It Wants?* contains 45 essays from *The Newsletter* that focused on better communication.

Dr. Dale was author of many books, including *How to Read a Newspaper* and *Audio Visual Methods in Teaching*, which was published in three editions and was translated into Spanish, Urdu, and Japanese. His *Living Word Vocabulary* with Joseph O'Rourke has remained a standard work in vocabulary knowledge.

He served on the Boards of Directors of the Division of Audio-Visual Instruction, National Education Association; the American Film Library Association, UNESCO; and Phi Delta Kappa.

He received many honors and awards, including the Ohio State Alumni Award for Distinguished Teaching; the Eastman Gold Medal Award from the Society of Modern Picture and Television Engineers; the Citation of Merit from the International Reading Association; and an honorary degree from Ohio State University.